Praise for Complex Simplicity

"Lucian Conway is a respected researcher and careful thinker. His academic work on cognitive complexity has attracted much scholarly attention and has extended our knowledge of cognitive complexity. He looks at issues in new and intriguing ways. Luke's academic research has relevance to not only everyday thinking, but also to issues as broad as prediction of wars and terrorist attacks. This book provides an engaging, fun, yet serious argument for the Christian worldview. Lucian Conway's book takes a new and refreshing perspective on arguments for faith. In the tradition of G.K. Chesterton, Lucian Conway presents his case in an entertaining, yet thought provoking manner."

~ Dr. Roger Tweed, Psychology Instructor, Kwantlen Polytechnic University, multi-published author.

"Dr. Conway's book successfully merges evidence-based psychological principles with Biblical principles, to create an evidence-based argument about the reality of our Christian God."

~ Dr. Shawn Reynolds, Clinical Psychologist, Nexus Psychology, Edmonton, Alberta, Canada.

"Truly an incredible read for seekers, skeptics, Christians, Atheists, and everyone in between! Complex Simplicity is intelligently written, thought-provoking, and will even have you laughing. Conway provides a refreshingly unique book in the apologetics literature."

~ Dr. Shannon C. Houck, Assistant Teaching Professor, Syracuse University, multi-published author.

Complex Simplicity

How Psychology Suggests Atheists Are Wrong About Christianity

Lucian Gideon Conway, III

Complex Simplicity
How Psychology Suggests Atheists Are Wrong About Christianity

Authored by Lucian Gideon Conway, III

Edited by S. E. Thomas, M.A.

Published by The Dramatic Pen Press, L.L.C.
Lolo, Montana

ISBN: 1-64157-000-8
ISBN-13: 978-1-64157-000-8

DEDICATION

For Kathrene and Autumn,

the best wife and best daughter

in the known universe.

ACKNOWLEDGEMENTS

I would like to sincerely thank the following people for their help in this collective enterprise. First, I am eternally grateful to my wife, Kathrene, for her endless patience, encouragement, love, and support during the writing of this book. Without her, this book would have been in the electronic trash heap a billion times over (and I'm pretty sure that's not even mathematically possible). She not only kept me from having exactly two hundred and four emotional meltdowns, she also patiently listened to hours and hours of complex simplicity talk and served as a great sounding board. I am also eternally grateful in an exactly parallel way (that's a big deal in our house) to my daughter, Autumn, who patiently listened to me tell her all the jokes in this book and laughed at all of them (including ones that didn't make it in the final version), sacrificed a lot of Star Wars movie time with her dad, and more generally was supportive and kind throughout, even when her appreciation segment turned out to be a run-on sentence.

On the professional front, this book would be of absolutely no value if it wasn't for the amazing talent, tireless work ethic, and ceaseless drive for perfection of my editor and publisher, Susan Thomas. I am immensely indebted to her for believing in this book enough to push it to be the very best it can be.

I would also like to thank five academic reviewers who dedicated their time and immense talents to reading all or part of this book and offering invaluable suggestions: Drs. Peter Suedfeld, Shawn Reynolds, Shannon Houck, Roger Tweed, and Greg Ganssle. All of the superb and thoughtful feedback I received helped make this book what it is today.

Finally, my life would be meaningless without the inspiration that ties it all together: Jesus, to whom I am indebted for this book – and for everything else in my life worth having.

CONTENTS

CHAPTER ONE

EVIDENCE OF THE WORKING MACHINE

When I was a child, our 1970 Oldsmobile sedan broke down, and my father took it as a personal challenge. Rather than paying a professional mechanic to fix it, my father—a college professor and accountant by trade—decided that he himself would replace the very small valve responsible for the problem. That sounds easy—but unfortunately, this valve was apparently buried deep within the engine, so he basically had to take the entire engine apart and put it back together. As a result, for months on end, our garage looked like the splayed guts of a Star Wars tauntaun[i]: The internal organs of our beloved Olds were strewn in haphazard ways in every direction. I was no Han Solo; I did not want to even stick my head in there. It seemed more likely that my father was going to create a cyborg or accidentally launch a nuclear attack at Vermont than he was going to get that Oldsmobile running.

And I will never forget the moment when he brought me to our garage to show me the end result. The car indeed looked fine—at least, it still had four tires and a hood, and it gave no appearances of having become an evil robotic intelligence or an exploding bomb. That was good. But it was not the car that caught my attention.

What caught my attention was the alarmingly large bucket of car parts in the corner. Yes, after months of taking apart the engine of our car and putting it back together—months spent replacing one tiny valve, which was the only part he had actually bought new to put into the car—after all of that, a giant bucket of parts was left in the corner. Mind you, these were parts that used to be in the car, parts presumably that the manufacturer of the car (whom I assume would be able to tell what parts were and were not necessary for it to function) thought were kind of important to make the car run. It was those parts my dad had failed to put back into the engine because he "could not figure out where they went." And now it was time to take the car out for its first post-splayed-tauntaun trial run. Let me tell you how I felt about getting in that car as a five-year-old kid.

---

[i] Kids: Google it. Adults: If you don't already know what this means, I'm sorry you had such a sad childhood.

I did not feel good about it at all.

Yet the amazing thing was this: When dad started the car up, it didn't explode, or launch a nuclear attack at a good-natured maple syrup farmer. The shocking truth is that it ran just fine. And it kept running fine for years after that.

Well, we can talk about fears and tauntauns and buckets of parts and bombs and cyborgs all we want, but *the ultimate measurement of whether or not someone really knows how to fix a car is whether or not the car works.* The standard of success is clear—the evidence is easy to interpret. And it turned out that my dad really did know what he was doing after all. If he didn't, our car would not have run.

I am an empiricist. I believe things on evidence. If we want to test a theory about whether or not something works, the best way to do that is to *see if it works.* And this book is primarily about testing the theory known as *Christianity.* Our primary question is: Does Christianity make the human machine run well? In other words, if I believe it and follow its advice, will I function according to my highest potential? As you will see, my primary method for answering this question is to provide a report from my own experiences and the experiences of other people I know – and to ask you to evaluate your own experience against that background.

Does Christianity make the human machine run well? If I believe it and follow its advice, will I function according to my highest potential?

Why This Book?

Give a man a fish and he will eat for a day; teach a man to fish and he will eat for a lifetime; give a man religion and he will die praying for a fish.
From *The Atheist's Bible*[1]

Religion is based, I think, primarily and mainly upon fear.... Fear is the basis of the whole thing—fear of the mysterious, fear of defeat, fear of death.
Bertrand Russell, *Why I am Not a Christian*[2]

We have this tendency to imagine that the primary debate between Christianity and Atheism happens on philosophical or logical grounds. But that really isn't so. Sure, some of the debates between (say) American Christians and Atheists are about the validity of the Ontological Argument for God's existence[ii], but a lot of what atheists say to attack religion isn't philosophical at all. Rather, a large percentage of it is actually an attack on the *effectiveness* of religion—on its *consequences.* Atheists do spend time discussing philosophical arguments, but they spend just as much time lambasting the negative consequences of religion. They argue (sometimes implicitly, sometimes explicitly) that Christianity breaks the human engine—and on those grounds, we should discard it.

A lot of what atheists say to attack religion isn't philosophical at all.

To illustrate, I went to an atheist website[3] that lists the top 10,000 atheist quotes by how many "likes" the quote has. (The top quote as of this writing had over 13,000 likes). I read through the opening page of fifty-two quotes—the most popularly liked atheist quotes according to atheists themselves—to find out how many of them focused on the *bad consequences* of religion versus how many of them focused on some more *academic-sounding intellectual argument.* And it was clear that more of them focused on bad consequences (50% by my count) than on philosophical arguments (31% by my count). Although this is just a small slice of the popular masses, it suggests that the average atheist seems to appreciate practical arguments more than intellectual ones.

And it isn't just typical atheists that seem focused on the practical, psychological side of things. As I write this, I have in front of me a stack of books written by atheists to denounce religion, including not only the atheist classic *Why I Am Not a Christian*[4] from Bertrand Russell—arguably the most famous philosopher of the last century (and unarguably still an atheist favorite, judging by quote "liking" counts)—but also some popular modern best-sellers from the group called the "New Atheists": *god is Not Great* by Hitchens,[5] *The God*

[ii] "Therefore, if that, than which nothing greater can be conceived, exists in the understanding alone, the very being, than which nothing greater can be conceived, is one, than which a greater can be conceived. But obviously this is impossible. Hence, there is no doubt that there exists a being, than which nothing greater can be conceived, and it exists both in the understanding and in reality" (St. Anselm, Archbishop of Cantebury, *Proslogium,* chapter II, p. 54).

Delusion by Dawkins,[6] *The Moral Arc* by Shermer,[7] *God and the Folly of Faith* by Stenger,[8] *God: The Most Unpleasant Character in All Fiction* by Barker,[9] and *Breaking the Spell* by Dennett.[10]

All of these books deal with philosophical arguments in varying degrees, sometimes countering arguments written for God's existence (such as the cosmological argument[iii] or the argument from the complexity of life[iv]), sometimes offering more proactive arguments against God's existence (such as the argument from religious pluralism[v]).

But all of those books also spend quite a bit of time ignoring philosophy and instead arguing that Christianity just plain doesn't *work*. *Every single one* of the modern atheist books I have read spends at least some time making a *psychological* case that Christianity is essentially *ineffective*. Consider just three title chapters from Hitchens' best-selling book *god is not Great*[11]: "Religion kills" (Chapter 2), "A note on health, on which religions can be hazardous" (Chapter 4), "Is religion child abuse?" (Chapter 16). Those chapters, and many others besides, are not really about the cosmological argument for God's existence or any particularly high-sounding philosophical stuff—they are rather about whether or not religion *works*. Hitchens thought it doesn't—he thought it kills you, is bad for your health, and is like child abuse.

[iii] "If our universe truly is contingent, the obtaining of certain fundamental facts or other will be unexplained within empirical theory, whatever the topological structure of contingent reality. An infinite regress of beings in or outside the spatiotemporal universe cannot forestall such a result. If there is to be an ultimate, or complete, explanation, it will have to ground in some way the most fundamental, contingent facts of the universe in a necessary being, something which has the reason for its existence within its own nature. It bears emphasis that such an unconditional explanation need not in any way compete with conditional, empirical explanations. Indeed, it is natural to suppose that empirical explanations will be subsumed within the larger structure of the complete explanation" (*Theism and Ultimate Explanation: The Necessary Shape of Contingency*. Timothy O'Connor, Oxford, Blackwell, 2008, 76).

[iv] "An irreducibly complex system *cannot* be produced ... by slight, successive modifications of a precursor system, because any precursor to an irreducibly complex system that is missing a part is by definition nonfunctional.... Since natural selection can only choose systems that are already working, if a biological system cannot be produced gradually it would have to arise as an integrated unit, in one fell swoop, for natural selection to have anything to act on" (Michael J. Behe 1996, 39; emphasis added).

[v] With so many religions in the world, how can you be sure yours is true? The argument based on the Hindu parable (from the Rigveda) of a group of blind men trying to identify an elephant by feel, but each can only feel one small part of the animal and, therefore, the various claims they make is only a partial truth.

Who Cares? Practical Arguments Matter

I am as firmly convinced that religions do harm as I am that they are untrue.
Bertrand Russell, *Why I Am Not a Christian*[12]

And it seems to me that it is largely on these practical grounds—and not on philosophical grounds—that the atheists are winning the cultural narrative. As indicated by the quotes from the previous section, atheists say that religion makes people work less hard because they spend time *praying* for the fish that they could instead be actually *catching* with a fishing rod, and the culture is starting to believe them. Atheists say that religion is a bad thing because it causes people to live in fear—and the culture starts absorbing it. As far as I can tell, it isn't so much because atheists came up with a new argument against God's existence—it is because they have been particularly effective at convincing people that believing in God is actually *bad* for you. And if a belief is *bad* for you, they assume it likely isn't true. Bertrand Russell's quote is appropriately illustrative of this approach, but it doesn't go far enough—it isn't just that religions do harm *and* that they are untrue; the implication is that religions do harm and *therefore* they are untrue.

Thus, the stakes are higher than a mere debate about the relationship between religion and hard work. And what have Christians done with the new atheist attack on the effectiveness of Christianity to keep the human engine purring? We have largely ignored it. Rather, Christians have spent considerable energy trying to rebuff the intellectual arguments of atheists based on science and philosophy; meanwhile the sweeping assertion that *religion is bad for people and societies* has been meet with comparative apathy, piecemeal rebuttals, or both. Quietly, alongside more formal philosophical arguments, atheists seem to have snuck in the apparent revelation that Christianity is bad for you, and rather than meet that attack head-on, we have responded by defending the *Ontological Argument* with ever-increasing fervor.

But this is a mistake. The average person doesn't base their decisions about religion on the current status of the *Ontological Argument*; they base it on what they believe happens to them in their real life. Atheists are explicitly waking up to this fact. Consider atheist Sam Harris' comments in his book *The Moral Landscape*:

Having received tens of thousands of letters and e-mails from people at every point on the continuum between faith and doubt, I can say with

> *confidence that a shared belief in the limitations of reason lies at the bottom of these cultural divides. Both sides believe that reason is powerless to answer the most important questions in human life.*[13]

> The average person doesn't base their decisions about religion on the current status of the *Ontological Argument*; they base it on what they believe happens to them in their real life.

Average people don't go in much for reason—they don't trust it. You may think I'm making fun of average people and writing yet another book about how to manipulate the public; on the contrary, I quite agree with average people. Oh, I do see value in *Cosmological Arguments* and *Special Design* and the *Complexity of Life*. It's important that what I believe at least makes philosophical and scientific sense, and we'll discuss in Chapter 3 how Christianity actually helps us better place these different ways of justifying knowledge in their proper epistemological places. However, taken alone with no other evidence, I find a lot of philosophy- and science-based apologetics on all sides largely non-persuasive. That is largely for one of two overlapping reasons.

(1) If an argument is based on scientific evidence, to trust it I'm required to trust the opinions of scientists. Scientists are great people who use excellent grammar and have well-groomed goatees—but as a scientist myself and as someone *inside* of the thing, so to speak, I don't trust scientists enough to base the ultimate state of my soul on what they say. If my faith is dependent on what a cosmologist says about quasars—if it is in the hands of the modern scientific zeitgeist about the complexity of DNA—then I think history suggests it is a shaky thing indeed. If I'm going to truly believe in something, I need more than that.

(2) If an argument is based on logical reasoning that serves as the basis for philosophy, I can see that logical reasoning is sometimes fallible. I love reason—but reason alone is a poor guide. This is in part because people don't always agree on what makes a reasonable argument. Our reasoning machines are often subjectively subservient to our experiences and intuitions. My friend Scott thinks the Ontological Argument for God's existence is an air-tight,

unbroachable reason to believe in God; I gave it an "F" when I graded arguments for God on my *Apologetic Professor* blog,[14] because I just can't imagine that if God cared that much about our *sheer belief in him* as such, He would hide the best proof in an obscure logical argument (as opposed to say, showing up in the sky for all to see and saying "here I am, believe in Me!"). Indeed, psychology research suggests that different cultural groups vary quite a bit in the degree that they endorse logical "principles."[15]

Reason is funny that way. If I came up with a set of logical arguments why aliens must exist, no matter how good those arguments are, part of you would feel like "yeah, but I haven't *seen* those guys, so what are we talking about?" Your personal experiences would trump the logic of my aliens theory. Likewise, you may come up with an argument that seems to point directly to God, but until I've actually had experiences that point to God—until I can see things in my own life that are consistent with the God theory—then at best, your argument will help me to keep my mind open to God, but it won't ultimately compel me.

What Should *the Religious Response Be?*

When Christians are not ignoring the practical psychological side, we are often dealing with the religion-is-bad-for-you argument in a piecemeal fashion. But this approach is doomed to be scattered and largely ineffective.

For example, it isn't enough to simply point out that there are Bible verses that directly contradict many of the assertions made by atheists, though it is often easy to do so. So I could simply say in response to the notion that *Christianity encourages inaction* that the Bible explicitly teaches the value of hard work (2 Thessalonians 3:10-14[16]), that Paul refused to accept money for his ministry and instead worked as a tentmaker (Acts 18:2-3), that the Bible explicitly says that action is better than faith –indeed, the Bible chastises people who claim to have faith but don't physically help people in need (James 2:14-17)—and that Jesus taught people to leave one's sacrifice at the altar in order to make things right with other people (Matthew 5:23-24). In fact, the opening quote of the previous section about religious people dying from lack of fish is rather odd in light of the fact that Jesus actually told a group of fishermen to re-cast their nets in the book of Luke

(5:4)—that is, he told them to take more direct *action*. I could also, in response to the notion that *Christianity is based on fear*, quote the book of First John (4:18), which says: "There is no fear in love. Perfect love drives out fear, because fear has to do with punishment. The one who fears is not made perfect in love." I could further point out that the most frequent command in the Bible (variously issued 366 times) is "Do not fear."

Those things are true enough, but that strategy would be largely ineffective for at least two separate reasons. (1) Atheists can rightly point to other Scripture verses that seem to focus on prayer or faith to the exclusion of action, or that could conceivably be used to induce fear. (2) Atheists can (with a sad but poignant truth that we would be fools to deny) point to poor examples from Christian history of people or cultures who used prayer as an excuse to avoid action, or who used fear to bludgeon people. I know some of those Christians myself personally. So basically we end up in a game we might call *What Point Do You Emphasize?* In this game, we are all looking at the same facts on both sides, but simply changing points of emphasis to suit our needs. Atheists emphasize one set of facts, we emphasize another, and the two sides never really dialogue at all.

No, what is needed is something more sweeping, something more fundamental. At its root, atheists don't merely claim Christianity is untrue; they claim it doesn't *work*—they claim Christianity is bad for people, and use that as evidence that Christianity's claims are false. And we, perhaps out of arrogance because we assume people won't *really* believe that (though they are clearly starting to!), perhaps out of a silent fear that the atheists are right and religion is an antiquated notion on par with a Roman aqueduct, have not responded to this sweeping attack with a sweeping rebuttal.

It would be colossally arrogant of me to claim this book to be quite the sweeping epic this grand introduction implies. So, in fine lowering-the-expectations fashion, I am not claiming that. However, I *do* hope it is a starting point—food for thought in the ongoing discussion about whether or not religion is good or bad for people. What I want is the same thing atheist Daniel Dennett wants in the introduction to his thoughtful book *Breaking the Spell*:

> *I realize that some people may feel about religion the way I feel about music. They may be right. Let's find out. That is, let's subject religion to the same sort of scientific inquiry that we have done with tobacco and*

alcohol and, for that matter, music. Let's find out why people love their religion, and what it's good for. And we should no more take the existing research to settle the issue than we should take the tobacco companies' campaigns about the safety of cigarette smoking at face value. Sure, religion saves lives. So does tobacco—ask those GIs for whom tobacco was an even greater comfort than religion during World War II, the Korean, War, and Vietnam.[17]

I also want that spirit of inquiry—let's start over and look at the whole question of whether or not Christianity works from a broad level. Let's open our minds and look at what we know about the human machine and about Christianity's effect on that machine. Let's decide if religion is like music—or like a tobacco ad.

What Is the Standard for Running Well?

I, of course, think Christianity is something glorious like music and not something crass and manipulative like a tobacco ad. As such, the primary goal of this book is this: I want you to see that, contrary to what a lot of atheists are currently saying, my experience teaches me that Christianity is very, very good at getting the human machine to run well.

What does it mean to *run well?* Successful human functioning involves roughly three different components. (1) When the human machine is working, people are **mentally connected with reality**. If you believe you can beat two-time MVP Steph Curry in a game of one-on-one, the way you think about your basketball skills could probably use a little tweaking. If you think you can lose weight by having *Mork and Mindy* TV marathons while you eat 600 pounds of donuts every day of your life, then you are not what psychologists would refer to as *a well-run epistemological ship*. If you think politicians are mostly telling the truth…you get the picture.

(2) Running well means **being happy**. A working human machine would not be a miserable, joyless black hole. When we are right, we lean towards happiness, and if some philosophy of life tended to produce misery wherever it went, I would not line up to endorse it as *making our engine purr like a kitten.*

(3) Running well means **being a productive and useful citizen**. A person can be a happy serial killer who knows they would lose to

Steph Curry in a game of one-on-one, and yet very few people would hold up that person and say "there's the human machine humming along – if only we could all be like that *serial killer*." So you are running well to the degree that you add value to the people around you. Ending up in jail – not good. Losing your job because you are lazy, or abandoning your family because you prefer to watch porn on the internet – these things exemplify a broken machine.

Standard for Running Well:

1.) Mentally Connected with Reality

2.) Happiness

3.) Being a Productive and Useful Citizen

Now, while I could spend six chapters telling you all about the standard for *running well*, I'm not going to do that. I am aware of the fact that these things are sometimes in tension, and this issue can be complicated. I teach classes on this tension – I know, for example, that it might make you happy to overindulge in eating food that a starving person needs, but it would not make you a good citizen. I also see that sometimes knowing the truth about things can make you unhappy.

Indeed, part of the point of this book is to demonstrate how Christianity helps bring all of these things together in a positive way. But I don't spend a lot of time right now on that point for two reasons: First, because this book is a response to atheists' attack on what I believe, and atheists and I entirely agree about the ultimate *goals* for a working human machine. You will see in these pages that atheists challenge Christianity on all three grounds – they think Christianity makes people lose touch with reality, that it makes people unhappy, and that it makes people immoral and unproductive citizens. I disagree with atheists about that, but the one thing we *agree on* is the standard of judgment, the *ends*. Atheists and I completely agree that anything that made someone lose touch with reality, consistently unhappy, and immoral would be a bad thing and doesn't make us *run well*. We simply disagree about whether my religion does or doesn't do those things.

Second, while I personally think having an audience of dolphins or tarantulas for this book would be top-drawer, I nonetheless imagine that you are a human being and that mostly you have a good sense in your own life of what makes people seem to work and what doesn't. Because I'm human too, I'm guessing we have roughly the same sense. But for the record, if you think a perfect life involves believing you can beat Steph Curry at one-on-one while being super-duper depressed all the time and ending up in jail for being a total jerk, then *this book isn't for you.* Otherwise, you can nobly carry on to the next section.

The Sample of One, Psychology, and Apologetics

Now maybe you are like me – maybe you tend to throw up your hands a bit at a lot of what Christian apologists, or Atheist apologists, or any kind of "ologists" say. And maybe you respond to this book by saying *great, another stupid apologetics book.* Maybe you'd be right about that.

And yet I think the method of this book nevertheless can contribute something useful to the discussion. Here's why. There is little that we know as well as we know ourselves – our own experiences. I am an empiricist in the classic sense that I trust what I see, feel, breathe, and think. And when it comes to the point, atheists' claim that my religion doesn't *work* simply does not meet my own experiences. I get their point; I see the difficulties; I do not blindly follow my religious creeds. And yet, it is my religion that is primarily responsible for my own sanity.

As such, this book will in part present to you a kind of open-book experiment on a sample of one: Myself. It will tell you why, in my own life, I do not think what the atheists say about my religion maps on to my own experiences. Those experiences suggest something rather different – they suggest a vast, complicated, psychological landscape that exists in myself and other people – a landscape that is predicted in broad brushstrokes by the *map* that Christianity claims to be. And contrary to what other people have told me would happen, when I use the map as a guide, I move along just fine.

You may reasonably reply that an empirical case study of one is hardly a worthy response to so grand a challenge; and you'd be right. But it turns out that it isn't just me. I focus on my own experiences because they are the ones I know best, and I respect that other people have had different experiences. But I also believe that a lot of evidence suggests my experiences are not *entirely* unique. Other people seem to have found the map useful, too.

And *that* subject falls under the purview of the modern science of *Psychology*. Psychology is the study of the human mind. It is the study of how and why we think and feel the way we do. It is the study of what makes the human machine *work* and what makes it *not work*. It goes beyond my sample of one to look at the larger picture of what is true of a lot of people.

It is also (by happy coincidence) my own area of scientific expertise. So part of this book will be a report from science about what it has to say about the human machine. In that sense, I am a conduit of information – and I plan to spend some time telling you that my science, far from being at odds with Christianity, actually largely supports it. This research is useful because it largely validates that I'm not (entirely) an anomaly; it isn't just me – it goes beyond me.

But you don't need to believe me – or science – or anything, to get the point I hope you will get out of this book. What I really want you to do is to look inside yourself and see if you feel the things I feel. If you don't, then pick up another book. For example, if you don't feel the tension (discussed in Chapter 4) between the joy of freedom and the obvious usefulness of boundaries, then this book isn't for you. But if you do feel some of the psychological tensions discussed in these pages, then this book is a challenge to you: It is a challenge to see that maybe, just maybe, in the same way Christianity makes sense of these things to me – in the same way that Christianity helps all the seemingly-disparate parts of my human machine function – that maybe, in that same way, it might help your machine function, too.

Now, my goal is *not* that, as you read this book, your machine would actually *work* better. I am not a clinical psychologist who sits people on a couch and has them talk about their childhood. I'm an experimental scientist. No; my goal is not so much to show you the path to personal happiness as it is to inspire you in some small way to consider faith. I want you to look inside yourself, not to make you happy, but to honestly evaluate – based on your own experience – what *would* make you happy, wise, and healthy. I want you to look back over your life, to think of your own inner workings and your own psychology, and honestly consider the question of what *would* make your machine work best. I don't think many of us really *try* Christianity because it is awfully inconvenient. But what if *you* did – would it work?

It works for me. And I'm going to try to convince you that it could work for you, too. And if that's true – if it honestly would work – then I think it's an important piece of evidence that it's actually true. After all, if Christianity is a life manual for fixing the human machine, then a primary piece of evidence for its genuine authority is that we *run well.*

The Scope of this Book

Anyone setting out to dispute anything ought always to begin by saying what he does not dispute. Beyond stating what he proposes to prove he should always state what he does not propose to prove.
G. K. Chesterton, *Orthodoxy*[18]

Like Chesterton, I think it is useful—though sometimes a trifle boring—to clarify exactly what you do *not* hope to accomplish in a book. So here let me do some due diligence, if for no other reason than I don't want readers to imagine I am claiming more than is reasonable from this exercise.

This Book is Not a Definitive Argument for the Truth of Christianity

An atheist doesn't have to be someone who thinks he has a proof that there can't be a god. He only has to be someone who believes that the evidence on the God question is at a similar level to the evidence on the werewolf question.
John McCarthy, from *The Atheist's Bible*[19]

On my blog, I have a series where I give each argument for God's existence a "letter" grade. And one of my favorite blog-ish sayings is this: *I do not believe there is such a thing as an "A" argument.* That is, I personally don't believe that there is a single argument that would convince all open-minded people at all times and all places of God's existence—if only they would read it and digest it.

Thus, I want to make clear that this book is not an attempt to convince you definitively that Christianity is true. I know it won't do that—and it shouldn't do that, if you are the open-minded person I hope you are.

In fact, it may surprise you to learn that I'm not even trying to persuade you that the atheists don't have a point. They do. I feel their point, too—some days more than others. I think almost all honest religious people question God at one point or another; this life does not always make sense and one rather imagines that God *would* make sense.

My aim is much more modest: I hope to persuade you that a lot of what modern atheists say about Christianity is *open for debate*. They are saying things that are going largely unchallenged, and I want to at least challenge them. If you are not a Christian, I have no illusions that this book will do the trick, but I hope it removes some mental obstacles, makes you *think* about the reasons you may or may not believe. As to your coming to believe, I'm not worried about that—that is literally out of my hands. (I of course believe it is in Someone else's hands, but let's not split hairs in Chapter One!).

I think almost all honest religious people question God at one point or another; this life does not always make sense and one rather imagines that God *would* make sense.

In other words, my aim isn't to bring the evidence on the God question up to the certainty you feel about, say, 2 + 2 = 4, but it *is* to bring it to a bit higher level than evidence on the *werewolf* question. Christianity claims that God not only came to earth, but that He left us with a practical guide for living. The sheer numbers who have reported the effectiveness of this guide ought to give pause to the skeptic. I'm agnostic about werewolves much like John McCarthy is, but I know of no werewolf that literally billions of people claim have written a life manual that effectively guides them as they work, love, parent, and eat donuts. I am a thinking skeptic, who in part came to Christianity by degrees because of *evidence*. So while I have plenty of ordinary doubts and questions about God like most people I know, and I can understand honest disbelief, I nonetheless do not believe the evidence on the God question is remotely in the same category as evidence on the werewolf question. To imagine it is seems an intellectual tragedy to me that's equally as bad as imagining that evidence on the God question is the same as evidence on the 2 + 2 = 4 question. And I hope to persuade you of that, too.

This Book Does Not Claim All These Principles Are Uniquely *Christian*

As we shall see, large parts of this book involve illustrating the complicated *match* between effective psychology and Christian truth or teaching. I take pains to demonstrate that Christianity does, in fact, teach the thing I'm claiming it teaches, but it is important to note that often other religious or irreligious beliefs systems would teach much the same thing. Doubtless, atheists would likely agree with many of the principles illustrated here (for example, the discussion of reasonable boundaries in Chapter 4).

This is actually what one would expect. If Christianity is a beacon of universal truth, I would be shocked to find that its principles were found nowhere else but in Christian circles. That is like saying that only mathematicians at Harvard could possibly recognize 2 + 2 = 4.

But it does raise the question: What is the added value of a book specific to the psychological successes of Christianity if it presents a vision that overlaps so much with other belief systems? I think there are two related answers to this question. First, the goal of this book is to counteract a general impression that Christianity is a practical psychological failure. That is contrasted with two things I am *not* trying to accomplish. (a) My goal is not to articulate a defense against the accusation that other religions (such as Buddhism) are practical psychological failures. While I think that in many instances, the accusations as applied to other religions are also ill-founded, I am a Christian – that is what I can authentically write about. If a Buddhist would write a similar book defending Buddhist psychology, I would buy it – but I am not qualified to write it. (b) My goal is also not to convince you that *atheism* is a failure—and it certainly isn't to say that atheists are bad people. (I know many of them are quite intelligent, honest, truth-seeking people who love their neighbors and families. Some of them even have good taste in Cajun food.) Rather, my goal is to defend Christianity against people who say it doesn't *work*. In short, I blame prominent atheists for this book: If atheists did not want an ardent defense of why Christianity works, then they should not have claimed so vigorously that it was a failure!

Secondly, while sometimes atheism and Christianity teach similar psychological principles, often they do not. When they do not – as in the debate over materialism (covered in Chapter 5)—it is worth pursuing the effects that the contrasting visions might have on human psychology. In those cases, I generally find that Christianity is more usefully complex than atheism—one of my reasons for rejecting atheism personally is that it is not complex or expansive enough—and because I believe this is true, I will naturally try to point out how their attacks are often more simple-minded than the thing we are accused of, and how I think a more complex view is a better match to reality. That's inevitable given any book designed to respond to a sweeping set of attacks, and unavoidable for a book that specifically aims to show that atheists often attack Christianity on too-simple grounds. But in the main, my goal is merely to rebut these attacks and not to tear down atheism *per se.*

It follows from this that I do not believe atheists are wrong about everything they say. As a skeptically-minded person myself who never fully accepted the common religious upbringing of my youth without evidence, I empathize with atheists—even though at this point in my life, I entirely disagree with them on the question that matters most to both of us. Often atheists are right in their criticism of religion, and I've defended them sometimes on my own blog.[20] Some arguments that Christians use are dumb, even some of my own arguments, and when that's the case, it is a service to humanity for atheists to point that out.

This Book Does Not Claim a Working Engine is the Only Source of Evidence for the Debate

One very reasonable reviewer of this book pointed out that it seems strange to hold the practical value of religion in such high esteem, given that its practical value could be independent of its truth value. After all, it is certainly possible for things that are demonstrably false to have positive consequences. It would definitely make me happy to believe in Santa Claus – but wanting it to be true does not make it true. To use our other criteria for *running well*, it is even possible for things that are false to both lead to a truer understanding of the world in some larger sense and to foster better behavior. It is very likely false that George Washington heroically admitted to his father that he had cut down a cherry tree in his childhood, but believing the cherry tree story is true might make me have a more generally accurate picture of the first U.S. President as the honest person he likely was. Believing that story is true might also inspire me to take ownership of my *own* behaviors in a positive way. Yet none of those positive consequences of the belief make it *true*.

There are a lot of possible sources of evidence relevant to the Christian/Atheist debates, and many of them have nothing to do with whether Christianity is psychologically functional. A belief in a *semi-omnipotent green frog that lives in my attic and loves me immensely* might offer positive psychological benefits, but it would (presumably) be false on other grounds. Those other grounds of evidence matter. I once wrote in a blog piece[21] that I personally believe in Jesus – and not, say, some other god like Osiris – on evidentiary grounds such as historical probability. That kind of evidence is important – but it goes beyond the scope of this book.

Thus, there are plenty of reasons I personally am a Christian that I'm simply not talking about here. But no book can cover every argument. And the particular (often overlooked) argument about a belief system's practical value is important. It is true that I would not believe in Christianity without some reasonable evidence that Jesus was a living person and that the Bible is historically viable. But it is equally true that, even if you could convince me that the Bible (say) presents a historically accurate picture of Jerusalem in the first century, I would probably not spend a lot of time reading it if I was sure its claims for *my* life would prove invalid. It is the second kind of argument that atheists have levied that is the subject of this book.

This Book Does Not Claim Christianity is Without Difficulties: The "I Don't Know" Problem

Skeptics like to point out that there are a lot of difficulties in the Bible. So let's just say up front: The skeptics are right. There *are* a lot of difficult bits in the Bible. Skeptics are also right to point out that Christians have historically engaged, and sometimes still engage, in horrible, mean-spirited, evil behaviors that have done a lot of harm in the world. That's true; they have and they do. It would be profoundly unhelpful for me to deny the horrors of religion—and I mean my own religion—or the truly oppressive things that Christianity has done when it has had political power.

I have no intent of glossing over Christianity's problem areas. Like Daniel Dennett, I think the thing needs to be judged in total, considering all the evidence we have on both sides.

And I admit up front that *I don't always know the answer.*

Now it turns out that there is a slippery slope for the phrase "I don't know." I teach a class to our incoming graduate students on how to teach, and we actually practice saying "I don't know" on the grounds that it is a good thing to honestly admit when you don't know something. On the other hand, I also point out to them that if they say "I don't know" to *every* question, their students will begin to think they are kind of dumb and not worth listening to, so if that happens a lot, maybe they should bone up a bit on the topic they are teaching.

So too here. I don't know what the exact tipping point is for being incapable of providing answers to questions before serious doubt should set in. But I do know that if you are a professor of quantum physics and I asked you "so what is the point of quantum physics" and you said "I don't know," I'd probably stop listening. So I do realize that if Christians can't answer some basic questions, you'd be reasonable to stop listening. And in this book, I focus on big-picture answers to the practical questions involved in getting the human machine to run well.

On the other hand, it is unreasonable to expect everyone to know everything. And while a lot of atheists subjectively appear to enjoy an open-minded comfort with *not* knowing things, they also occasionally (in what sometimes feels like a double standard) discuss the Christian's inability to answer every difficulty as if this failure is extremely problematic.

For example, Richard Dawkins mockingly said in *The God Delusion*: "Do those people who hold up the Bible as an inspiration to moral rectitude have the slightest notion of what is actually written in it?"[22] The implication is that I could not possibly believe in the Bible if I was aware of all that it said—that I am ignoring the difficult bits entirely.

Well, take comfort, Dr. Dawkins. It turns out that I do have (more than) the slightest notion of what is in it. I have read the Bible almost every day of my life since I was in my twenties; I have taken multiple classes on its teachings; I have read the parts that cause people angst; I am *fully aware* of what is in it. And yes, there are plenty of passages in the Bible I don't understand—plenty of passages that have hurt my faith—plenty of passages that have made me question whether or not it was a truth-telling thing. I am completely aware of those passages—and yet I believe in the Bible anyway.

Why? Well, I don't believe in it blindly. I believe in it for the same reason that Richard Dawkins believes in Darwinian evolution, even though some evidence points against it (such as the sudden biological advances creatures seem to make in the fossil record after long periods of biological stability). That is, I take the whole of the picture—the sum of the evidence—and I use that. Richard Dawkins does not throw out science because scientific consensus for years accepted fake evidence for evolution now known as *Piltdown Man.*[vi] Nor should he. I do not throw out Darwinism because (last time I checked) Darwinists themselves cannot seem to figure out how something as complex as a basic cell could have evolved. I do not throw out relativity theory because I cannot understand why, if time travel is theoretically possible, I have not yet seen it.

And I do not throw out the Bible because I cannot entirely figure out why God ordered children killed in the Old Testament—and yet the New Testament says violence is so bad that even an angry thought is on par with murder. As with science and evolution and relativity theory, I look at the whole picture—and the whole picture suggests to me that (unlike what atheists sometimes say) the God of the Bible isn't some kind of child-killing monster. I don't understand everything He does, and some of it confuses and even appalls me—but what I *do* understand suggests He is compassionate and loving and kind, holy and just and honest. Thus, I am willing to assume that whatever the Old Testament passages mean, they don't mean that God hates children. I am willing to admit that I don't fully understand what they *do* mean, but I take those kinds of passages in light of the overall picture. I treat them the way scientists might treat things about their own science that seem contradictory or that they don't understand – I try to figure them out; I try to push the apparent contradictions to gain knowledge; but I don't immediately throw out the entire theory in question.

Consider a different analogy: Imagine that, after gaining a lifetime of evidence that your best friend is an honest and trustworthy person, you hear they told a bold-face lie to the police about an important murder investigation. Do you immediately throw out all the accumulated evidence that your friend is honest and assume your

---

[vi] Although the *Piltdown Man* fossil was always the subject of much controversy and debate, scientific consensus nonetheless largely accepted it initially as valid, and it was displayed in the prestigious *British Museum* for many years as legitimate scientific evidence. Its influence was so widespread that it was used 13 years after its introduction by Clarence Darrow as evidence for evolution in the famous *Scopes Monkey Trial.*

friend is guilty of a moral tragedy? I'd guess not. Rather, you'd more likely assume that you don't know all the facts about their behavior in this instance. You might assume that – if you could know all the facts – it is possible your friend didn't lie at all; or that, if they did lie, it was for a perfectly defensible reason. Not knowing all the facts, you would probably be upset and want to investigate, but you would also likely approach the investigation with the background knowledge of years of evidence about your friend's good character. In the case of God, we by definition do not have access to even a small percentage of the facts – God knows everything *about* everything, and we are in comparison almost knowledge-less. So when I read in the Bible over and over that God is just, and then I see things that make me question the Bible's view of Him as just, I think it is in part reasonable to realize I don't always have all the facts, and the appearance of unfairness might result from of my own lack of knowledge.

I think it is in part reasonable to realize I don't always have all the facts.

Of course, that is dependent on first establishing the larger picture about what the Bible actually does teach. In this book, we'll first (in Chapters 2-7) look at some of the pieces to this picture, and then in our concluding chapter, we'll return to this larger issue of how the whole thing fits together.

Complex Simplicity:
The Christian Vision for the Running of the Human Machine

A car engine is a very complex thing, full of interlocking parts. If one of those parts goes wrong – even one small ten dollar valve – the whole machine could break. And yet when the machine is running well, the experience of it is quite simple. A working complex car engine makes my life simpler, because I do not have to carry all the bags from the grocery store the five miles from my house. When that complicated engine purrs, my experience of driving the car itself is beautifully simple.

This is a picture of the Christian vision for human psychology, and that picture captures what I mean in this book by *complex simplicity*: Christianity makes *life* simpler by providing a manual for how to build the complex human machine. A lot of things in life are like that. Complex beliefs, paradoxically, can make the experience of life simpler. Consider the algebraic expression "17000n=51000." To the person who does not understand the complex logic of algebra, the expression will forever remain a complex mystery, full of rather large numbers and mystifying expressions. It is only the person who understands the logic of algebra, who has a complex belief system *prior to* experiencing reality, who can believe with simple authority "n = 3."

G. K. Chesterton said: "A stick might fit a hole or a stone a hollow by accident. But a key and a lock are both complex. And if a key fits a lock, you know it is the right key." [23] But note this. Yes, a key and a lock are both complex. But, once you've got the right key for the right lock, opening a door with it is the simplest thing in the world. It is the person who tries to enter a door with an (admittedly) much simpler nail file who will find the practical experience of opening the door complex. The person with the right key need only slide the key in and turn it.

Like a mechanic who knows the complexity of an engine or a locksmith who knows the complexity of a lock, I believe Jesus knows the complexities of the human machine—and that, as a result, His teachings make that human engine *run* and run *well.*

A key and a lock are both complex. But, once you've got the right key for the right lock, opening a door with it is the simplest thing in the world.

The Complexity of Human Psychology

Oh, Truth, Truth, how inwardly even then did the marrow of my soul sigh for Thee when, frequently and in manifold ways, in numerous and vast books, they sounded out Thy name though it was only a sound!

St. Augustine, *Confessions*[24]

Life is often complex, even when we don't think of it that way. The farmer sows at one point and reaps at another. That is complexity; that is differentiating between unlike things, for sowing and reaping are different things. If the farmer used a simpler strategy—merely sowing all the time, sowing even when her crops were ready to harvest—she would not be a very good farmer.

Now of course one doesn't have to have a Ph.D. in complexity theory, or even be a complex thinker, to engage in these sorts of complexities. We do it all the time without a great deal of effort. We naturally treat a 1-year-old differently than a 30-year-old. We learn quite easily to distinguish the phonemic sound in "look" from the sound in "Luke," and do not often think that the phrase "look out the window" is a command to hurl the unfortunate Luke outside into the cold bitter world. We know shoes go on our feet and hats go on our heads; that is, they serve different purposes.

Given the complexities of life in general, it should come as no surprise that the 100 billion interconnected cells we call the *brain* contains quite a bit of complexity. The resulting subjective experience known as the human *psyche*, our conscious experience, is quite a mystery to unravel. How are we to make such a complex tangle of conflicting emotions and imperfect reason work as it should? The claim of this book is that Christianity fits the complexity of the human psyche like a hand fits a glove or a key fits a lock. Human psychology is multi-faceted and expansive, and Christianity meets this multi-faceted psychology with multi-faceted teaching. It does not attempt to put a nail file in a keyhole, or fix a complicated engine without understanding how it works.

Indeed, human psychology is full of complex tensions. Sometimes we want to show mercy to a homeless person, but we worry we might actually be doing them more harm than good. Sometimes we want to feel like we are a unique individual, but we worry that we won't fit in with our friends. Sometimes we feel the sneaking suspicion that the beauty of a violin points to another world, but then we feel the annoyance of a very real headache in *this* world.

Christianity provides a roadmap for understanding all these diverse experiences, and as such helps the human machine run well. Its vision is expansive and complex. In this book, my primary method for illustrating this idea is this: In each chapter, we will discuss two sometimes-opposing elements in the human psyche. And then we will discuss how Christianity accounts for and integrates these two elements—how it attempts the grand experiment of keeping all the good parts of the human psyche—and by so doing, keeps our human engine purring. In all cases, I argue that following the Christian prescription for complex integration is a formula (so to speak) for psychological health. We can go wrong in many ways—we can go wrong by being too simple on either side of each psychological dilemma. Christianity aims to keep the whole, and in helping us integrate the different parts of our complex psyche, shows us how to run simply and run well.

Are Christians Simple-Minded?

We are a nation that is unenlightened because of religion. I do believe that. I think religion stops people from thinking.[25]
Bill Maher

Of course, upon hearing all this talk about Christianity prescribing complex integration for psychological health, the pragmatist (influenced by talking heads like Bill Maher) might reply: "It's all well and good for you to talk about how complex Christianity is and how Christ produces complexity—but it's all bluster because Christians are, in actual fact, simple-minded people. So all this talk about Christianity producing complex integration is shown to be the lie it is by the reality of what Christians are actually like."

Now, if it turned out that Christians really *are* simple-minded (we'll return to the empirical question a bit later), Maher might be making a reasonable argument, but I also think it is not strictly necessary to the main point I want to make in this little book. Why? Just like scientists do not always adhere to scientific principles, or like environmentalists do not always recycle, Christians do not always actually follow Christianity. The question I am technically pursuing in this book is not "what is the average Christian like?" but "if one followed Christian teachings fervently, what would the psychological outcome be?" Although we will of course talk quite a bit about average Christians – because one assumes that the average Christian is more likely to follow Christianity than

Just like scientists do not always adhere to scientific principles, or like environmentalists do not always recycle, Christians do not always actually follow Christianity.

the average atheist – there sometimes will be variability in the degree that pockets of Christianity follow Christ.

That said, I have a lot of sympathy with the pragmatist who dismisses the notion of *Christian complexity* because she perceives that Christians themselves are simple folk. And in fact, the reader will no doubt notice that this book is primarily about the *effect* that Christianity has on people, and thus it is a bit hypocritical of me to ignore the larger effect it has on the complexity of how people think. Further, to some degree it is a bit too convenient for me to use evidence about differences between average Christians and non-Christians (as we do in Chapter 4) when it suits the argument, but avoid it otherwise. Thus, though not strictly necessary, I think it is important to address the question of whether or not Christians are, in fact, the simple-minded bumpkins we are made out to be.

I do research on complexity for a living, and the short answer is that Bill Maher is wrong. (I know it is hard to believe that a *news media personality* is wrong about something, but life is full of surprises). Let's talk about this evidence in a bit more depth.

How is Complexity Measured?

Complexity can be measured in a number of different ways. For example, I could just ask you to report how complex you think you are. And sometimes psychologists do that. But of course, we know people are biased in their perceptions of complexity[26] and also motivated to think of themselves highly, so you might imagine yourself to be Immanuel Kant (among the most intellectually complex people we have ever scored) when you are actually Bill O'Reilly or Bill Maher (both very low by our own scientific scoring). Thus it is probably a good idea to utilize a more objective measurement of how complex people are.

In my field, the primary way we test for complexity is to score open-ended responses for the underlying dimensional structure of the statements. These statements can literally be anything on earth that is (or can be) written down – transcribed speeches, books, essays, answers to specific questions during research sessions, poems, song lyrics, movies, even my mother's e-mails. Using this scoring method, statements with only one dimension are low in complexity, statements with multiple dimensions are higher, statements where those dimensions are integrated together are higher still. This highly-validated scientific measurement of complexity, drawn from the seminal work of Peter Suedfeld, is called *integrative complexity*.[27,28]

To illustrate, consider the topic *broccoli*. You might say that *broccoli tastes terrible*. That would not only mean that you have excellent taste—it would also mean you are low in complexity on that topic. That statement has one dimension (taste) associated with one target (broccoli)—that is in fact the lowest possible complexity. Contrast that with the statement *broccoli has a terrible flavor, but it has a nice texture*. (I realize you probably cannot believe broccoli has a nice *anything*—but work with me here). That statement incorporates two dimensions—taste *and* texture. So it is more complex than just saying broccoli tastes bad.

Scoring complexity is more involved than that, but this example illustrates the basic idea. So below, when I refer to *complexity*, that's what I mean. I mean that statements from real people who did not know they were being measured for complexity are assigned scores by expert coders (or by computer systems designed by experts) to measure the dimensional structure of their statements. This method of measuring complexity is so important that it has been used to predict the outbreak of war,[29,30] the behavior of terrorists,[31] successful or unsuccessful therapy,[32] the outcomes of elections,[33] and when people are telling a lie[34]—to name just a small handful of its scientific accomplishments.

Evidence that Christians are Not Simple-Minded

Using this integrative complexity method, a number of studies have looked at the relationship between Christian belief and complexity. For example, our lab has coded the complexity of three famous Christians who converted from atheism, as well as two famous atheists who abandoned Christianity for atheism. We were interested in comparing the effect of *renouncing* Christianity with the effect of *converting to* Christianity. The upshot of that work is that there was certainly no tendency for the two atheists (including Robert Price) to become more complex after they left Christianity, while two of three Christians (including C. S. Lewis) showed an increase in complexity after conversion.[35]

A follow-up study looked at C.S. Lewis' private letters in greater depth. Did becoming a Christian make C.S. Lewis simple-minded? No. Actually, research clearly shows that Lewis became *more* complex after his conversion to Christianity, and that this change was true within both non-religious *and* religious topics.[36,37] We've also compared the State of the Union Speeches of extremely religious U.S. presidents (such as George W. Bush and Jimmy Carter) to less religious ones, a comparison which showed they were basically the same in terms of complexity.[38]

More recently, we've compared famous Christian intellectuals with equally-famous counterpart atheist intellectuals for how complex they are. For example, in one study,[39] we compared three Christian intellectuals with three atheist intellectuals who lived in roughly the same era. These "matched" pairs served as rough comparisons between elite Christian and elite atheist intellectuals. From the early 1900's generation, we scored Atheist Robert Blatchford (his famous book *God and my Neighbor*) and Christian G. K. Chesterton (his famous book *Orthodoxy*). From the mid-1900's generation, we scored Atheist Bertrand Russell (his famous book *Why I am not a Christian*) and Christian C. S. Lewis (his famous book *Mere Christianity*). From the 2000's generation, we scored a 2006 debate between Atheist Richard Dawkins and Christian David Quinn.

It is worth noting that Blatchford and Chesterton were direct intellectual opponents (and indeed the coded books were actually part of a kind of ongoing debate between them), and Dawkins and Quinn appeared opposite each other in the very debate we coded. Lewis and Russell were not direct opponents, but were the most famous intellectual representatives of Christianity and atheism of their era.

The results of this test showed that in each case, the Christian was more complex than the counterpart atheist, and the overall *Christians higher than Atheists effect* met the typical standards of science (probability that the effect was due to chance = .003).

We have also looked at larger populations of laypersons. In one study looking at almost 40,000 persons in the U.S. who were writing about the value they most believed in, the use of religious language was significantly positively correlated (probability that the effect was due to chance < .001) with the essay's integrative complexity.[40] People who value religion in this sample thus were on average *more* complex than those who valued it less.

In another study, people were divided into whether they were orthodox Christians and non-orthodox Christians by a validated self-report questionnaire (the "non-orthodox" category potentially included both non-Christians and less orthodox Christians). Then all participants across two studies were asked to respond to religious prompts (life after death or the existence of God) or non-religious prompts (the death penalty or free trade between U.S. and Canada). These responses were scored for complexity. Orthodox Christians were lower in complexity than the non-orthodox, but only for religious topics; for non-religious topics, they were equal in complexity.[41] Although this study did not compare Christians with atheists (but rather compared more versus less orthodox religious people), this nonetheless suggests that under some circumstances, more religious people *can* be simpler than less religious people – a point we return to in a minute.

That study also used a very limited range of topics. Another study of over 500 people compared fundamentalist Christians (who presumably ought to be the simplest sort of Christians) to non-fundamentalists on a much larger range of topics that included religious questions (such as being asked to comment on the degree to which religion is necessary for a good life) and non-religious questions (such as the death penalty, alcohol use, tobacco use). In this study, no overall difference emerged between fundamentalists and their non-fundamentalist counterparts; instead, fundamentalists were lower in complexity on some topics (as before, most typically those topics associated with religion) but higher on others.[42]

Are Atheists Simple?

Taken in total, research to date suggests that holding devoutly to the Christian religion either (1) does not affect overall complexity or (2) increases it. There are and always will be exceptions, but the tenor of the work so far is not remotely consistent with the idea that Christians are generally more simple-minded.

Am I saying that *atheists* are simple-minded? Am I arguing that Christians are *more* complex than non-Christians? The answer is no on both counts. In actual fact, I don't believe Christians are, on average, *more* complex than (say) atheists. So it was never my intent here to demonstrate that. At a research level, it is possible that Christians are more complex in these samples, not from the influence of Christianity *per se*, but from the fact that Christianity has traditionally been the most normative belief system, and that itself can sometimes make people more complex.[43] Personally, I know plenty of perfectly reasonable, complex-thinking atheists, and if you are one of those, do not imagine that I am trying to insult you. Our own data would show that atheists are sometimes *more* complex than Christians, and sometimes *less* complex.

My aim was instead more modest. It was to combat the pragmatist who would dismiss the rest of this book because she assumes Christians in reality are *simple* people. That is untrue as I see it. Christians are at least as complex as most other sorts of people, so the argument that Christianity is in actual fact *creating* simplicity does not get off the ground. Whatever lens you look through the current research with, these data do not support a "Christians are simple" framing.

In reality, I'm not sure it is quite right in any event to expect Christianity, operating perfectly, to make people more complex about *everything*. This is for several reasons. (1) A lot of research—including a lot of our own research—shows that one of the best predictors of complexity is the topic domain.[44] (By "topic domain" I mean what the complexity is about. Most people, for example, have higher complexity about the topic "alcohol" than about the topic "coeducation," and that's true regardless of their religious or political orientation). And research suggests that it's hard to talk about *any* group of people being more complex, writ large, than another group of people, because some groups are more complex on some topics but less complex on other topics.[45] (2) We'll see in the next chapter that there are reasons why people might be *reasonably* more closed-minded on some topics. For example, I would not want anyone to have a complex view on the issue of *murdering people for fun*—I would hope you would simply say "nope, that's a bad idea at all times and in all places." If you have a more complex view like "sometimes it's bad to murder people for fun, but hey-ho, sometimes it's ok"—well, don't expect an invitation to my birthday party anytime soon. (3) A perfectly-operating truth vessel would see things as they *are*. While human psychology is generally complex, some things *are* simple—and although not the focus of this book, it is certainly possible for us to *over*estimate the amount of complexity in our environment.[46]

As a result, I actually would not expect, even if all Christians followed Christian teachings perfectly, that they would be more complex on *every* topic than everyone else *all the time*. They wouldn't. So my goal here was never to prove that they were. However, I hope I have invalidated the idea that Christianity is some kind of cult-like, simplicity-producing thing *as a whole*. It isn't. Blaise Pascal and St. Thomas Aquinas and St. Augustine and Descartes were all devout, Church-going Christians, and I have not heard it said that their Christianity made them into simple-minded folk. And there are thousands upon countless thousands of Christian intellectuals stretched out across time, intellectuals recognized as brilliant (see Chapter Five for a partial list) by essentially everyone (Christian and non-Christian alike). At some point, it becomes rather absurd to say that this Christian system, which has historically spawned so much intellectual complexity of high value and continues to do so today, is actually (as Bill Maher claims) "stopping people from thinking."

Now, with those caveats out of the way, we can get on with the larger point of this book: To illustrate how Christianity helps us integrate complex psychology into a working machine – a machine with a complex mechanism but a simple outcome.

At some point, it becomes rather absurd to say that this Christian system, which has historically spawned so much intellectual complexity of high value and continues to do so today, is actually (as Bill Maher claims) "stopping people from thinking."

CHAPTER TWO

OPEN-MINDEDNESS MEETS CLOSED-MINDEDNESS: THE PSYCHOLOGY OF BELIEF

Imagine that you believed American society existed for two primary purposes: To create the *McDonald's Chicken McNugget* and to produce the glorious musical stylings of *Billy Ray Cyrus*. In my opinion, that would not be a particularly implausible set of twin beliefs. I once ate a Chicken McNugget that had literally been sitting in a trash heap in the back seat of my Nissan Sentra for *nine months*. And I remember saying to myself after I ate it: *Even after nine-months of trash-heap sun exposure, that chicken nugget has STILL GOT IT! Take THAT, France! No freakin' croissant would have tasted that good for that long.* And let's be honest, there is nothing quite like a good solid dose of Billy Ray Cyrus' rock anthem *Could've Been Me.* I'm pretty sure I would faint with giddy delight if I ever tried to listen to Billy Ray *while* eating a Chicken McNugget.

Now here's my point. Having that set of beliefs is, by definition, narrow-minded. All beliefs are exclusionary. If you believe the Chicken McNugget is the food pinnacle of American civilization, you are not also free to believe the Burger King Whopper is the pinnacle (heresy!). If you believe our very best musical talent is Billy Ray Cyrus, you are not also free to believe that Justin Bieber is the cat's musical meow (horrid!).

It doesn't matter what belief you put in [X], having belief [X] is, by definition, exclusionary. To have a belief *at all* is to psychologically narrow the scope of accepted reality. That is true of a belief in chicken nuggets; it's true of a belief in the Second Law of Thermodynamics; it is true of atheism. If you are a materialist atheist, your belief system narrows the scope of your accepted reality to exclude God and a spiritual afterlife. This sort of exclusivity is, of course, also true of Christian belief. If you are a Christian, as I am, you have a narrow set of beliefs in the sense that anyone who believes

To have a belief *at all* is to psychologically narrow the scope of accepted reality.

anything has a narrow set of beliefs. But that means nothing more or nothing less than this: If you believe Christianity is true, you believe it.

Are Christians Too Closed-Minded or Too Open-Minded?

So far as I can tell, there is not one word in the Gospels in favor of intelligence.
Bertrand Russell, from *The Atheist's Bible*[1]

The inspiration of the Bible depends upon the ignorance of him who reads.
Robert G. Ingersoll, from *The Atheist's Bible*[2]

All thinking men are atheists.
Ernest Hemingway, from *The Atheist's Bible*[3]

Some atheists seem to think Christians are rather stupid and narrow-minded. And they don't just think we are narrow in the sense that all beliefs position the believer to be exclusive, as explained above—a lot of atheists clearly think Christians are *uniquely* idiotic. They think Christianity itself is a system that produces closed-minded people who shut out all rational thought and refuse to look at reality as the complicated morass it is.

On the other hand, one of the peculiar things about Christianity is that it has been accused of being both too simple and too complex. Yes, Christians are often painted by the modern world as simple yokels who refuse to acknowledge subtle scientific complexities and the necessity for the progression of truth; we are accused of having a too closed-minded attachment to antiquated notions. But we are also often attacked for believing incomprehensible, contradictory theories and for being too open about accepting those contradictions. Consider these words by prominent atheists:

When I ask those believers to give me the context of a troublesome passage, they often produce a verse from another part of the bible—sometimes written centuries later in another language and country with a different agenda—such as "whoever does not love does not know God, for God is love (1 John 4:8, written in Greek around the year 100 C. E.). Rather than seeing this rebuttal verse as

contradictory and anachronistic, they pretend that it explains and justifies the crime against humanity they are trying to excuse.
Dan Barker, *God: The Most Unpleasant Character in All Fiction*[4]

If hellfire is the stick, mystery is the carrot. The propositions to be believed ought to be baffling!... For a truly awesome and mind-teasing proposition, there is nothing that beats a paradox eagerly avowed.
Daniel Dennett, *Breaking the Spell*[5]

In struggling to reconcile the inherent contradictions of their faith, Christian thinkers, in the finest traditions of a political spin doctor, convey negative images to their flock, who, without thinking, accept them as, well, the gospel truth.
Vincent Bugliosi, *Divinity of Doubt: The God Question*[6]

Barker, Dennett, and Bugliosi all claim Christians believe things that seem, to them, contradictory and paradoxical. Worse, they claim we believe them *without thinking*. We "avow" them "eagerly." So Christians are, in a sense, accused of believing in an incredibly complex system with an extremely simple faith.

I do not dispute this characterization of Christianity *per se*. I rather dispute the moral implication that it is a bad thing in every circumstance. I do not dispute that Christianity encourages a simple-minded faith in what can sometimes be a set of complex beliefs. But I argue that this is precisely the way things should be, perhaps the way things *have* to be. I find that saying this is a bad state of affairs is like saying it is bad for an algebra professor to believe, with a simple-minded ferocity, the mathematical assumptions underlying that glorious enterprise, while simultaneously (on the basis of those believed assumptions) working out very complex calculations.

The combination of simple, closed-minded faith and complex, open-minded beliefs underlies many great institutions in this world, academic or otherwise. And I would argue, too, that it *should* (and often does) underlie the operation of the Christian church. As we will see in the coming chapters, Christians believe things that sometimes seem to be in tension with each other—things such as that God is very close to us and very distant from us *at the same time*. That is a complex belief—and yet we strive to hold that belief with a simple faith. Allowing for both sides of that psychological coin is complicated—but it only works if you actually *believe it*.

> The combination of simple, closed-minded faith and complex, open-minded beliefs underlies many great institutions in this world, academic or otherwise.

Of course, it would be nonsense to hold a simple faith in a system that produces massive complexities if the system itself is totally wrong, or the things it produces simply do not work. And I do get that this is part of the atheists' point. So if, as is claimed, our complex system is based on falsehoods—or the contradictions are so difficult that no reconciliation is possible—then, of course, it is a silly enterprise to hold a simple faith in it. One would indeed be insane to believe that the Western Grey Horned Toad had both four horns and no horns—such a claim would suggest to me that the animal probably wasn't real after all. And it would hardly be noble to discuss the complexities of the Western Grey Horned Toad's genetic structure if, in fact, by all human knowledge, the Western Grey Horned Toad did not exist.

Throughout this book, I will show how the complexities inherent in Christian teaching also map on to the complexities in human psychology. Thus, I hope to at least give you pause in your belief that the complexities we produce are, like our fabled horned toad, a figment of our imagination. For the moment, though, I want to focus our attention on Christianity's psychology of belief itself. As we shall see, the Church is unabashedly open-minded, and for that we make no apologies. But our combination of open-mindedness and closed-mindedness saves us from falling into disastrous errors that lie in *mere* closed-mindedness or *mere* open-mindedness as such.

In the remainder of this chapter, I discuss both sides of this coin and how they fit together within Christianity. We start on the side on which we are most often attacked—but which is easiest to defend.

The Surprising Virtues of Closed-Mindedness

This is the highest point of philosophy, to be simple and wise.
St. John Chrysostom[7]

Christ appeared not as a philosopher or a doctor of so many words, or as one who disputed noisily, nor yet as a scribe renowned for wisdom and learning; but in the

utmost simplicity did He talk with men, showing unto them the way of truth in His life, His virtues, and His miracles.
Bl. Angela of Foligno[8]

People are always praising the virtues of "open-mindedness." It is a wonderful trick, really, a delightful example of linguistic egoism run wild. The term at face value suggests that the open-minded person is willing to explore all options, to truly look at other viewpoints. But my own observation suggests that, in its everyday usage, it means the exact opposite of this. When someone refers to the "open-minded" person they often mean "a person who agrees with my opinions." When my uncle used to say of his hometown "this is a great city, it's full of open-minded people," he actually meant "this city is full of people who aren't racist"—for one of his strong opinions was that racism is wrong. But he has smuggled the closed-minded truth into his rhetoric: He obviously believed his opinion was more correct and enlightened than other viewpoints. After all, no "open-minded" person could believe otherwise.

> When someone refers to the "open-minded" person they often mean "a person who agrees with my opinions."

Believing all persons should hold to one opinion (by amazing coincidence, your own) is very closed-minded indeed. The more one believes one's own opinion is right—the more one is unwilling to entertain the possibility that her own opinion is wrong—the more closed-minded one is. That is what being closed-minded means: To not consider alternative viewpoints as potentially valid.

Open-mindedness means exploring options; closed-mindedness means settling on one, and refusing the others. The very phrase "all open-minded people should believe *A*" is thus contradictory, because open-minded people would (by definition) refuse to settle on *A* (or *B*).

The raw, real kind of closed-mindedness is not, necessarily, a bad thing. My uncle was a closed-minded and simple man, perhaps the most closed minded man I have ever met. You may think this an insult; I think it a compliment. My uncle refused to consider—even for a moment—the possibility that racism ever has any legitimate justification. He would not surrender, not for anything in the entire world, the banner that shouts "all persons are created equal." You see, he did not have an open mind in this area. It is a trait I admired in him.

To say he had closed his mind on the possibility of legitimate racism—well, it is hard to imagine a higher compliment.

Be Careful Where You Point That Thing

Set your minds on things above, not on earthly things.
Colossians 3:2

You will keep in perfect peace those whose minds are steadfast,
because they trust in you.
Isaiah 26:3

The sensitive reader may well respond, "Well, it's all very well and good to be closed-minded about something like racism; but oftentimes people are closed-minded about truly bad things. Racists themselves are closed-minded when they should be open-minded." And now we have come to the key point. Yes, closed-mindedness *can* be a bad thing, but it can also be a good thing. The same sharp point that slices your hand can also slice the tomatoes for dinner. What it's *pointed at* is of utmost importance. Closed-mindedness is the same way. It is a grand thing to closed-mindedly accept a truly right ideal. In fact, that is perhaps the primary intellectual goal of life. But it is a truly wicked thing to closed-mindedly accept a truly wicked ideal.

Thus, open-mindedness is only a good thing under certain circumstances. Let me provide a few examples from research in my own discipline of psychology. I suppose it goes without saying that slavery is absolutely wrong. In antebellum America, the Northerners by and large opposed slavery, while Southerners typically supported it. Hopefully we can agree that the Northerners were right and the Southerners wrong about this particular moral question. Their disagreement, however, caused no small amount of tension between the political leaders of the two groups.

Sometimes talk of war broke out. Each side possessed a few complex thinkers: leaders of a decidedly open-minded disposition. The Southern leaders of this ilk said "well, of course slavery must be defended and all, but, really, we must consider it in the context of many factors. After all it is a complex problem." Open-minded Northern leaders likewise said "you know, slavery is wrong, but we must consider the pros and cons of going to war." And, indeed, in the compromise of 1850, as they say, cooler heads prevailed. Thus war was averted, as war is often averted, by listening to the open-minded persons.

But the open minds were not the only voices; they were merely the early winners in the political struggle. Other, less complex voices had been silenced in the compromise of 1850. They would rise again. These closed-minded sorts of leaders, too, existed on both sides. The closed-minded Southern leaders said, "Slavery is right—I don't care if we have to go to war to defend it; it's our right to have it, and it must be protected at all costs." The closed-minded Northern leaders said, "Slavery is wrong—I don't care if we have to go to war to stop it; it's totally wrong and must be ended."

These closed-minded people on each side eventually drove the United States into a Civil War, a war that cost the lives of more Americans than all the other U.S. wars combined.[9] But I would contend this. Those Northern leaders who, in their great complexity, argued for open-mindedness and compromise were very likely wrong. Their complexity steered them astray. In stark contrast, those Northern leaders who doggedly refused compromise with the evil of slavery were very likely right.[vii] It was thus very likely closed-mindedness that saved the country from slavery.

It Is Better to be Open-Minded... If You're Wrong

Then he opened their minds so they could understand the Scriptures.
Luke 24:45

[vii] I am aware that this narrative is an oversimplification of the Civil War in many ways. Not all Northerners who drove the country to war were secessionists; not all Southerners who stood firm were in favor of slavery. Further, it is not entirely clear what would have happened had the peaceful elements won out and thus no war had happened. It is possible that many of the negative consequences that resulted from the war could have been averted, and slavery could have been peacefully abolished at some later time without those negative consequences (and thus, it is possible that a better overall outcome would have emerged without the war). However, such counterfactuals are always impossible to know and in this case are nothing more than fairly vague conjecture. Other counterfactuals are equally as likely: It is also possible, for example, that without the Civil War we might still have slavery today in the U.S., and that this pro-slavery U.S. attitude would have grown with American influence to spread overseas, in much the way that American economic approaches have grown and spread. All of that is sheer guesswork. What we *do* know is what actually happened – we know that slavery was, in fact, ultimately abolished because abolitionists were willing to fight to see that through. And those abolitionists were, according to research, simple-minded people.

They know nothing, they understand nothing; their eyes are plastered over so they cannot see, and their minds closed so they cannot understand. No one stops to think, no one has the knowledge or understanding to say, "Half of it I used for fuel; I even baked bread over its coals, I roasted meat and I ate. Shall I make a detestable thing from what is left? Shall I bow down to a block of wood"?
Isaiah 44:18-19

I emphasize the possible positive power of closed-mindedness because I believe you already appreciate its negative power. Obviously—as I am sure you've already noticed—the converse is true as well: open-mindedness can also be of great benefit. For example, if you believe a block of wood is a god, it would be better for you to follow the advice in the Book of Isaiah to "stop and think" and open your closed mind. Likewise, the Southerners who doggedly defended slavery at any cost were greater fools than those who would have offered a more complex—a more open-minded—solution. If you believe slavery is a good thing, it is better if you are open-minded about it. Open-mindedness is thus best if you believe incorrectly, and closed-mindedness is best if you believe correctly. Perhaps you see where this is leading. But let's look at another example first.

> Open-mindedness is thus best if you believe incorrectly, and closed-mindedness is best if you believe correctly.

In the 1930's, Neville Chamberlain was Prime Minister of Britain. He was an extremely complex and open-minded sort of fellow. Thus, when Hitler began to be too aggressive, Chamberlain naturally employed a complex strategy of appeasement. To say the least, his attempts to evade conflict failed dreadfully. Later, his political opponent—the extremely simple-minded Winston Churchill—became Prime Minister. Churchill, by contrast, followed a very simple strategy in dealing with Hitler: You are a bad man, and we will not give you what you want. In fact, we think you are so bad, we will fight to avoid giving you what you want.[10]

Most historians would agree that Churchill was right and Chamberlain was wrong. Indeed, had Churchill's simple strategy been enacted earlier, it is possible that much tragedy might have been averted. While historical counterfactuals are impossible to know for sure, what we do know is this: The closed-mindedness he exhibited surely did help lead to the resolution of the war and put an end to the atrocities that had been occurring during the Holocaust.

Closed-mindedness accomplished its goal only because the *ideal* persons closed their minds around was, itself, good. If the ideal is bad, closed-mindedness is also bad. Take another example from Winston Churchill. Later in his life as Prime Minister, he was faced with a difficult situation in India concerning Indian independence. He was a simple fellow, and he maintained his usual lack of complexity in his response to that situation. He didn't consider the many subtle difficulties associated with the problem, nor did he try to work with the Indian officials. He simply said "no—India is our territory and we will just keep things as they are." Only in this case his simplicity didn't work. According to the judgment of history, he should have offered a more complex—a more open-minded—solution. He did not and, therefore, in this situation, his closed-mindedness hindered him.[11]

The End Goal Is Being Right

The point here is this: Being open-minded or closed-minded, as an end goal, is irrelevant. Being *right* is the thing that matters. Open-mindedness is only good in so much as it helps us *arrive* at the right conclusion. Closed-mindedness is only good in so much as it helps us *stay* with the right conclusion. But neither is a useful goal in and of itself.

Of course, it should be noted that, to the degree that one state of mind is inherently better than the other, closed-mindedness is clearly of a higher moral quality than open-mindedness. After all, in a moral progression, being closed-minded on *good* ideals, doggedly clinging to those things that are right no matter what is a good goal. In contrast, open-mindedness should never be the desired end goal. No one can say, in good moral conscience: "I want to be open-minded about truth.

Open-mindedness is only good in so much as it helps us *arrive* at the right conclusion. Closed-mindedness is only good in so much as it helps us *stay* with the right conclusion.

I want to believe true things when they're easy to defend, but when things get rough—poof! I'm tossing truth aside."

Holding On to Open-Mindedness

Still, I know, there is something in you that wants to hold on to the open-minded ideal. I know that because there is something in me, too. I want to keep being open-minded for two related reasons. First, the world is a complex place, truth is complex, life is complex, religion is complex; therefore, ought not I to be complex as well? Secondly, I know I am often wrong. Therefore, a certain amount of healthy self-skepticism is the mark of a truth-seeking person. In fact, this kind of skepticism is a key part of the Christian atmosphere (as we will discuss in a moment). So, my goal in this chapter is not to make you an entirely closed-minded person. Rather, my goal is to overcome what I guess is your natural bias towards thinking that open-mindedness is inherently a better state than closed-mindedness. That idea is, at any rate, entirely contradicted by the facts of history and human experience—if you believe open-mindedness is unilaterally better, you hold a kind of belief hypocrisy that Christianity calls you out of. In making this case, I hope you will think more complexly about complexity itself: That you will realize that sometimes complexity is good, but at other times simplicity is better.

Consider for an instant the possibility that Christianity is true. Now imagine Christ, given to die for the sins of the world, setting his mind (as the Scripture says) toward his appointed death in Jerusalem. What if he had been more open-minded about it? What if, in that moment in Gethsemane, he had pondered too long any other course of action except "Thy will be done?" We have discussed how closed-mindedness may have saved America from a future of slavery. We have discussed how closed-mindedness may have saved Europe from being overrun by Nazis. If Christianity is true, the closed-mindedness of one man quite literally saved the world.

Combining Closed-Mindedness and Open-Mindedness

If Christianity were something we were making up, of course we could make it easier. But it is not. We cannot compete, in simplicity, with people who are

inventing religions. How could we? We are dealing with Fact. Of course anyone can be simple if he has no facts to bother about.
C. S. Lewis[12]

When once one believes in a creed, one is proud of its complexity, as scientists are proud of the complexity of science. It shows how rich it is in discoveries. If it is right at all, it is a compliment to say that it's elaborately right.
G. K. Chesterton[13]

Although our view of the sublimest things is limited and weak, it is most pleasant to be able to catch but a glimpse of them.
St. Thomas Aquinas[14]

The house of my soul is too narrow for Thee to come in to me; let it be enlarged by Thee.
St. Augustine, *Confessions*[15]

I have spent some considerable pains challenging the modern intellectual dogma that open-mindedness is always better than closed-mindedness. The truth, ironically, is much more complex than that simple statement. The truth is that sometimes open-minded complexity is better, but sometimes closed-minded simplicity is better. Given this, it becomes important to parse out how open-mindedness and closed-mindedness ought to fit *together*.

Below, we discuss two different ways in which Christianity explicitly attempts to address the tension between these two aspects of the psychology of belief. And it is important to realize that this tension isn't restricted to Christianity itself—it is within *belief of anything.* Christianity doesn't create the tension between open-mindedness and closed-mindedness, but I believe it offers a set of solutions that help the human machine run well.

Oh, Those Unreasonable Reasonable People

Let's start by considering one of the questions that is at the fulcrum of closed-mindedness and open-mindedness: How are we to deal with the fact that knowledge means belief in some absolute truth, yet at the same time honest persons will recognize that there is some possibility they may be wrong? This admission leaves a lot of wiggle room. To paraphrase a famous philosopher whose name I've forgotten: "All reasonable people believe that their opinions are true in some sense. All reasonable people also believe that some of their opinions will turn out, in the end, to be false. So, all reasonable people believe that their opinions are true, but some of them are false. Frankly, I expected better of reasonable people."

How are we to deal with the fact that knowledge means belief in some absolute truth, yet at the same time honest persons will recognize that there is some possibility they may be wrong?

Christianity addresses both sides of this ancient dilemma. Like all reasonable things, the Christian belief system has some non-negotiable first principles. There *are* things Christians must believe in to be Christians. For example, the literal death and literal resurrection of Jesus Christ are basic Christian tenets. These absolute claims are surprisingly few, in the end—but they are there. One cannot get on without them; they define our faith. So, no one is denying that there are specific, non-negotiable beliefs. We return to those specific beliefs in a moment.

But there is also, aside from all that, a whole other set of beliefs which are not necessarily fundamental, and on which Christians have historically differed, and differed widely. What are we to do with these beliefs (say, about the interpretation of the first passage of Genesis, or about the application of Biblical principles to drinking wine)? The answer of Christianity to this problem may surprise some people, even some Christians. It is a very complex problem, and Christianity provides a very complex open-mindedness as a solution. That solution meets the two separate parts of the human psyche mentioned earlier—both the part that says we ought to *close our mind around true things*, and the other part that says we ought to be *skeptical of the things we claim to know*.

That Christian solution is essentially that, on these issues of lesser importance, people may work out their faith in different ways—and that these differences are to be fully tolerated. The classic example comes from Romans, where Paul says: "One man considers one day more sacred than another; another man considers every day alike. Each one should be convinced in his own mind. He who regards one day as special, does so to the Lord. He who eats meat, eats to the Lord, for he gives thanks to God; and he who abstains, does so to the Lord and gives thanks to God." It is clear: People may seek and arrive at different conclusions, and God will respect them for their different conclusions. This is fine; don't trouble yourselves about it.

That is why some of the statements in the Bible may seem confusing—even contradictory—to those outside of the faith. For example, the Apostle Paul says in 1 Corinthians "knowledge puffs up…if any man thinks he knows anything, he knows nothing yet as he ought to know" and later prays that the Philippians' love will "abound yet more and more in knowledge and all judgment." Now, on the surface, these statements may seem to contradict each other. Why should we hope to abound in knowledge if it is bad for us? But they don't contradict each other. Knowledge may be useful, knowledge may be attainable, knowledge may be real, knowledge may be straight from God. But it is simply an acknowledgment of what we see in our everyday lives to say that knowledge can be morally dangerous. One may be fully justified in his claim to knowledge, but this very self-assuredness is also often a sure path to that most deadly of sins, pride. This is why Christianity has always encouraged a healthy self-skepticism. We believe in the creeds—the foundational beliefs of Christianity—unashamedly; we think them true and other things not true. But to walk around acting like we've got it all figured out and other people don't—well, that is spiritual suicide. Christ's primary command to us isn't "think you understand everything." It is "love God and love your neighbor."

At a more purely informational level, we are explicitly told that we know only in part, that reality as we understand it will eventually cease to exist, that we currently see many things as "through a glass darkly" (1 Corinthians 13:12). These clear teachings of Christianity are not necessarily evident if one's only exposure to Christian teaching occurs through televangelists or Richard Dawkins. But be clear: We are instructed to pursue knowledge, to desire wisdom like farmland cracked with drought needs rain, and yet to view knowledge itself as incomplete and morally dangerous. That is why St. Thomas Aquinas, one of the greatest thinkers of all time, could equally say that "the ultimate end of man is to understand God"[16] and also reflect back on his own works with extreme skepticism: "The end of my labors has come; all that I have written appears to me as so much straw after the things that have been revealed to me."[17]

So, in this way Christianity clearly combines open-mindedness with closed-mindedness. We are encouraged to take Scripture seriously, to believe the creeds with undying devotion, but to be skeptical of that knowledge as mere knowledge. It is believing, with simple faith, that the creeds are true, while believing, on the other hand, that such knowledge, left as pure knowledge, can lead to a moral decline.

Is Christianity a Chicken McNugget or an Algebra Equation?

I opened this chapter by presenting a belief that is *unlikely* to be true: The Chicken McNugget is the apex of American food culture. Along the way, we have also discussed beliefs that are *likely* to be true: For example, the reduction of an algebra equation using basic math. My goal here isn't to convince you that Christianity is more like algebra than a Chicken McNugget; it is rather to open your mind to the possibility that Christianity's approach to belief itself is a reasonable combination of open-minded and closed-minded elements. While this reasonable combination can be seen in many other branches of human life (and thus I am not claiming it is unique to Christianity) – such as science – it is nonetheless not often associated with my faith. Yet the Christian vision is to keep both open-mindedness and closed-mindedness in all their positive glory. Christianity encourages the common sense notion that closing one's mind around a good ideal is praiseworthy, but it also encourages us to be humble in our knowledge, to realize its limitations, and to not value it too highly. Like an auto mechanic with a complicated knowledge of a complicated engine, Jesus helps the epistemological parts of the human belief machine hum.

CHAPTER THREE

AUTHORITY MEETS THE SCIENTIFIC METHOD: THE PSYCHOLOGY OF KNOWLEDGE

Sometimes you can learn more about what people truly believe from their actions than their words. I may *say*, in fine Book-of-Daniel-fashion, that I think a healthy diet is more important than a tastes-good diet, but my sincere devotion to that belief might be reasonably questioned by the people who watched me eat twenty-one donuts in a single morning. (That was a great morning, but a less-great afternoon).

Christianity often helps us understand, not just the psychology of those things that most people *say* they believe, but also the psychology of those things that most people *act like* they believe. In a sense, Christianity gets behind the curtain of our words; it offers a theory that accounts more fully for *all* the parts of our psychology.

The subject of this chapter is one such case: a case of an epistemological hypocrisy explained. The things people often claim they use in constructing their knowledge are not the things that they actually use. Or, better said—people *do* build knowledge on the things they claim to build knowledge on, but lurking in the background are often things that they *do not* claim. Christianity teaches that both the claimed and unclaimed things are legitimate: As I will show in this chapter, Christianity explains the psychology of knowledge in a way that incorporates what people do, and not just what they say they do. Just like Christianity might argue that both my claimed desire for health and my unclaimed desire for joyous eating are legitimate—and thus account for both my explicit and implicit psychological beliefs in a coherent way—so, too, does Christianity help explain the ways that people learn, whether they claim those ways or not.

This is easiest to understand in the context of the debate about religion and science, and it is to that debate we turn next.

The Religion of Atheist Daniel Dennett

But where are the examples of religious orthodoxy being simply abandoned in the face of irresistible evidence? Again and again in science, yesterday's heresies have become today's new orthodoxies. No religion exhibits this pattern in history.
Daniel Dennett[1]

Daniel Dennett and I are both religious. We both have unqualified faith in some things. In fact, often we have unqualified faith in the *same* subset of things. He believes strongly in the positivistic view of truth: "Yes," Dennett comments, "inquiry is a matter of getting something we want: The truth about something that matters to us, if all goes as it should."[2] I also believe in this view of truth. He believes with religious fervor that the Holocaust happened during World War II. So do I. We have not acquired definitive proof that our beliefs are true, yet we believe them. Neither of us experienced the Holocaust firsthand, yet we are sure it happened.

So Dennett and I share some common ground. Where we differ is not so much with how we acquire our beliefs but on a few specific beliefs themselves. I would say, for example, that God exists and loves everyone unconditionally, that He took on human form in the person of Jesus Christ to die for and thus save the world, and that life is found in His risen body and Holy Spirit. Dennett would disagree with those statements. On the other hand, by his own testimony, Dennett holds the following beliefs[3]:

"Life first emerged on the planet more than three billion years ago."

"Jack Ruby shot and killed Lee Harvey Oswald at 11:21 A.M., Dallas time, November 22, 1963."

Dennett doesn't just believe these statements in the general "that's my opinion and they are probably true" sense; he believes them with religious passion. He says (and I quote)[4]: "These are truths about events that really happened. Their denials are falsehoods. No sane philosopher has ever thought otherwise...." Now, I would not disagree with those statements as fervently as Dennett would probably disagree with mine. In fact, if asked to give my opinion, I would say that the 3 billion year guess is probably about right, and the Jack Ruby statement is 99% certain to be right. But that is irrelevant. The point here isn't to challenge Dennett on these particular beliefs, but to ask why he believes them so strongly.

Everyone, including famous, smart philosophers like Daniel Dennett, hold beliefs they cannot directly verify. I doubt he was around 3 billion years ago. I doubt very much whether he even has the necessary scientific training to properly evaluate the evidence first-hand. Unless I'm mistaken, he did not personally witness Ruby's shot and Oswald's death, nor undertake an investigation into the identities of the two men or the event itself. So where did those beliefs come from? How can we be confident in them?

Everyone, including famous, smart philosophers like Daniel Dennett, hold beliefs they cannot directly verify.

Dennett claims—as scientists everywhere claim—that he believes them because of a strictly empirical approach to science. That is, these statements are believable as true because they have been validated by empirical methods. And he thus attacks religion because we fail to attend to reality: We are not empirical, and that is why (the implication is) we are so often wrong.

This is a legitimate and thoughtful attack on Christian belief that I take quite seriously. All the same, I think it is based largely on three false assumptions. Namely, (1) Christianity relies on authority to the exclusion of other methods, (2) science uses empirical methods exclusively, and (3) non-empirical ways of knowing are inferior. All three of these assumptions are false. The truth is, as we shall see, that Christianity offers a more appropriately complex atmosphere that incorporates all ways of knowing proportional to their real value. And in so doing, it gets us behind the curtain of such simple claims about where knowledge comes from, and into the *actual* ways people acquire knowledge.

Authority versus the Scientific Method

There are a great many ways people acquire knowledge. Philosophical and psychology types have lumped them together under several large umbrellas (I'm especially indebted here to Brett Pelham[5]). For the sake of making my argument as easy to digest as possible, I'm going to discuss two larger approaches to knowledge that are at the fulcrum of our current discussion: Relying on Authority and the Scientific Method. The particular taxonomy we might use is not relevant to the argument—it's the larger contrast that I want you to see. However the argument is framed, the conclusions of this chapter remain the same.

Authority, Shared Common Sense, and the Scientific Method

Common Sense: Good sense and sound judgment in practical matters.
From the Oxford Dictionary.

One of the most pervasive justifications for our knowledge involves appeals to authority. When we rely on authority, we trust (for example) that someone who is an expert knows better than us, and we believe what they say. The majority of our knowledge comes from trusting authority – I believe, for example, that the sun is comprised of 75% hydrogen because competent scientists have told me that it is, and I trust them.

In contrast, sometimes our knowledge comes from common sense practicality that does not appeal to any specific authority figure. When the writers of the Declaration of Independence said *we hold these truths to be self-evident*, they were appealing to this kind of common sense. They assumed that you already had the *good sense and sound judgment* built into you, and that you'd perceive the value of (say) equality without needing an external authority to tell it to you. To take a different example, my guess is that you would not consider it *sound judgment* to stick a flaming porcupine up your nose, and thus I doubt you would feel the need to rely on external authority in making that decision.

Of course, *common* sense implies sound judgments that people *share together* (in "common"). When we say "someone has no common sense" in everyday parlance, we generally mean that they don't have the same sense that all normal people have. The Declaration of Independence writers presumably did not just mean that those truths were self-evident only to themselves; the argument would have little validity unless those truths were *widely* self-evident to a lot of people. I would assume that most people in most places would not think it wise to stick large, prickly animals up their nose. Thus, a lot of our own judgments are influenced by a kind of practical common sense that is assumed to be valid to most people.

This kind of shared common sense can take many forms and has influenced many different systems of knowledge acquisition. One of the most important of those is important for our present purpose; it is most typically referred to as the *scientific method.*[viii] The *scientific method* is defined by Oxford Dictionary as "a method or procedure that has characterized natural science since the 17th century, consisting in systematic observation, measurement, and experiment, and the formulation, testing, and modification of hypotheses." This method is based first and foremost on the common sense notion that we should believe in the power of our own eyes and ears. If I tell you there is a two-foot-long spider in the hallway of my house, and you want to know if I am telling the truth, the scientific method begins with making the effort *to go look in the hall.* It ignores the whole question of whether or not I have any authority to tell you about spiders; to the purveyor of the scientific method, it would not matter (in theory) if I were considered the world's greatest expert on spider size. Instead, it relies on the power of direct observation.

That is not all there is to the scientific method, of course: If I observe a spider while I'm in a drunken stupor, I most likely will not learn a lot from the experience about its specific size. That qualification would fall more under the category of what philosophers and psychologists have termed *logic* or *reason* than it would under direct empirical observation. But that and other qualifications also have an air of common sense about them, and it is beyond our present purpose to discuss all those qualifications in detail. The key point is this: The scientific method is a combination of many different forms of knowing (an issue we return to below) – but it begins with the common sense idea that I can trust my own eyes or sense experiences, and is infused with pragmatic common sense throughout. And this method is often contrasted with an over-reliance on authority.[ix]

[viii] The relationship between the notion of common sense and the scientific method is complicated. Common sense could be described as a shared intuition that results from shared experiences. In that way, empirical methods such as those used in science are similar to common sense because it is assumed that common sense results in part from cumulative shared experiences. For example, I assume that I would not shove a porcupine up my nose because I have enough cumulative experiences that tell me (a) the porcupine will not fit, (b) prickly things such as the porcupine hurt, and (c) my nose is sensitive. That is itself a judgment based on common sense empiricism. However, while recognizing the many points of overlap of these various epistemological sources in the present chapter, our focus is simply to compare and contrast those elements that are directly relevant to the modern attack on Christianity.

[ix] The categories used in this chapter are of necessity oversimplified. For example, reliance on authority and reliance on shared common sense share many psychological properties: (1) they are both largely automatic and heuristic in nature, and (2) people trust expert authority in part because our cumulative observational experiences tell us this method

Into the Expansive Christian Horizon

What counts as evidence for a person is whatever raises the likelihood for that person that the claim is true. Evidence is, as we said, truth conducive. Evidence for God's existence (or non-existence) does not have to be restricted to empirical findings discernible in the sciences, although some empirical findings might serve as evidence.
Gregory Ganssle, Yale University Philosophy Professor[6]

Now the mistake people often make—and that Dennett makes—when thinking about science and religion, is to assume religion focuses exclusively on authority, and science focuses exclusively on shared common sense notions like those in the *scientific method.* This isn't true at all. In fact, the truth is far more complex than this; the truth is that both science and religion use multiple ways of knowing. As Gregory Ganssle rightly recognizes in the above quote, contrary to the common assumption that religion relies solely on authority, it does not exclusively do so. Indeed, it relies very heavily on common sense appeals of all kinds, including direct empirical[x] evidence.

False Assumption #1: Christianity Relies Exclusively on Authority to the Exclusion of Shared Common Sense

I cannot believe in a God who has neither humor nor common sense.
W. Somerset Maugham, from *The Atheist's Bible*[7]

In my experience, people seem to think Christianity is about listening to orders from a Higher Power, that it is about taking dictation from a Divine Boss and doing what He says whether it makes

---

works. I am aware of both the psychological and philosophical overlap (e.g., I am aware of taxonomies comparing reason/logic, authority, perception/observation, and intuition). However, the larger point of this chapter would remain unaffected by whatever specific taxonomy we overlay on the discussion. The particular approach of this chapter was motivated by the specific attack that has been levied against my religion, which largely contrasts a reliance on authority with other forms of knowing, and secondarily challenges parts of common sense psychology. The potentially complicated nuances of the specific terms are not directly relevant to the response to this attack.

[x] I use the terms "empirical" and "observational" to refer to evidence primarily the result of our own sensory experience.

sense to us or not. And so my religion sometimes is, but genuine faith is more than that.

One of the reasons I believe in Christianity is that what God tells me to do largely makes sense to me. Like famous British author Somerset Maugham, I cannot believe in a God who has no common sense. I have a hard time imagining a world where what I believe is good or true is precisely the opposite of what a good God would tell me to do. If God made me, He'd have planted somewhere inside of me more or less the same moral and practical common sense He has.

I have a hard time imagining a world where what I believe is good or true is precisely the opposite of what a good God would tell me to do.

Say Ribbit?

Religion is about turning untested belief into unshakeable truth through the power of institutions and the passage of time.
Richard Dawkins, from *The Atheist's Bible*[8]

Critics of Christianity sometimes act like Jesus came to people and ordered them to hit themselves over the head with a Bible until they could convince themselves of its truth. If all you knew about Christianity was what Richard Dawkins said about it, you would probably believe that Jesus came to people and said: "You must accept what I say without evidence. If I tell you that *God is a big green frog*, then I expect you to say…*ribbit, ribbit*."

But it is not so. Yes, Jesus claims the divine authority to tell us what to do—that's true. Christianity relies more explicitly on authority than some other systems of belief. Consider that we believe the Bible because we think it a divine revelation—that is, we intuitively trust that it has proper *authority*. I believe in Jesus Christ's teachings because I trust that He (as the observers in the Bible say) "doesn't teach as one of the teachers of the law, but as one who has authority." Even more, I believe that the persons who wrote down the accounts of Jesus did so with moderate accuracy and that the story has been passed down through the years with moderate accuracy; all of this I accept because

I simply *trust* Christian authority.[xi] This trust is explicitly a part of my faith, and I am not in the least ashamed of it. (I will return in a minute to the issue of whether this is an inferior type of knowing.)

But, contrary to popular myth, Jesus doesn't ask us to believe in Him solely by *fiat*. In fact, a lot of what He does in the New Testament accounts is to call people back to their *own* common sense. He tells them not to believe in some new moral law that God has sent or some new fact that they must just accept, but rather to be more true to what their own common sense would tell them to do.

Evidence that Jesus Relied on Shared Common Sense

It would be an understatement to say that Jesus' reliance on shared common sense can be seen repeatedly in the Bible. In Luke 13:15-16, Jesus is criticized for healing someone on the Sabbath because it goes against religious tradition. And Jesus responds with an appeal to common sense: "Doesn't each of you on the Sabbath untie your ox or donkey from the stall and lead it out to give it water? Then should not this woman, a daughter of Abraham, whom Satan has kept bound for eighteen long years, be set free on the Sabbath day from what bound her?"

Do you see what Jesus is doing? He is arguing with them on the basis of principles that he assumes they themselves *already possess*. He doesn't tell them "I am God so do what I say," but rather "you *already* know that this woman's health is more important than your donkey's—listen to your *own* common sense!"

Jesus does this a *lot* in the Biblical narratives. In one particularly powerful passage (Matthew 23:23), he lists a number of ways that religious leaders were being hypocritical: "Woe to you, you teachers of the law, you hypocrites! You give a tenth of your spices—mint, dill, and cumin—but you have neglected the more important matters of the law—justice, mercy, and faithfulness." Our own common sense says something is wrong with us if we care more about superficial rules of giving spices than about heartfelt mercy and real justice. I don't have to think very hard to realize that, if I give a tenth of my income to the church and yet cheat my poor neighbor out of the tiny bit of land she

---

[xi] I am not here making an argument for a belief in the accuracy of the Bible. That argument is beyond the scope of this book. Here, I am only discussing the issue as an example of the general idea that the Christian approach to knowledge does include appeals to authority.

needs to live, I'm not behaving in a morally acceptable way. Something is radically wrong. My own common sense tells me so.

And Jesus tells them—he tells *all of us*—to attend to that common sense. And he doesn't stop there: He uses similar arguments to persuade people that the *quality* of a religion is more important than mere *conversion* to religion (Matthew 23:15), the temple is more important than the gold comprising the temple (Matthew 23:16), and that the true condition of their spiritual lives is more important than how they look to other people (Matthew 23:25-28). These arguments call us back to our common sense—to stop ignoring those parts of us that tell us that private reality is more important than public perception. It is easy to get caught up in superficial rules and in what other people think. It is easy to push down that common sense. But Jesus repeatedly wants us to attend to it.

Jesus often calls us back to our own common sense in more implicit—but no less profound—ways. It's interesting, for example, that Jesus frequently appeals to our sense of right and wrong by asking *questions* of the ordinary people around him, or by asking them to consider on their own what they think. For example, Jesus says: "Two people owed him five hundred denarii, and the other fifty. Neither of them had the money to pay him back, so he forgave the debts of both. Now which of them will love him more?" (Luke 7:41-42). In being asked about how to obtain eternal life, Jesus responded: "What is written in the law? How do you read it?" (Luke 11:26). In the famous parable of the Good Samaritan (Luke 11: 36), Jesus asks: "Which of these three do you think was a neighbor to the man who fell in the hands of robbers?" Elsewhere (Luke 6:9), Jesus, in challenging their hypocritical view of the Sabbath, says: "I ask you, which is lawful on the Sabbath: To do good or to do evil, to save life or to destroy it?" In a passage on not worrying (Luke 12:25), he asks them to consider the following: "Who of you by worrying can add one hour to his life?"

Jesus frequently appeals to our sense of right and wrong by asking *questions* of the ordinary people around him, or by asking them to consider on their own what they think.

I could go on. In all these discussions, Jesus calls us back to our own deeper common sense—a common sense that, as we'll see in

Chapter 4, we all too often ignore because it is inconvenient. He asks people to reach inside themselves to see whether or not love is increased by forgiveness, whether loving God and neighbor really are less important than minor points of the law, and whether the good one can do on the Sabbath is less important than the superficial rule. These are common sense principles his hearers would understand *already*, and Jesus is constantly drawing them out of us with stories, parables, proddings, and—sometimes—outright accusations of blatant hypocrisy.

> Jesus calls us back to our own deeper common sense—a common sense that we all too often ignore because it is inconvenient.

Do People Have a Shared Moral Common Sense?

It is possible that a skeptic might respond to this by criticizing Christianity for relying on the shared common sense *too* much. I once had this friend in high school (who we'll call "Billy" for the sake of anonymity) that, on a dare, bit a metal car key in half. Now I'm not sure what you imagine will happen when you bite a key in half, but what happened to Billy was this: It ripped his face up on one side. Some fool then dared the now-bleeding Billy to try to bite another key in half, using the *other* side of his mouth. And Billy did that straight away, which…ripped up the other side of his face.

While I do not want to slight this incredible achievement – after all, Billy did manage to *bite two keys clean in half* – this example made me wonder if my friend might not be fully stocked in the common sense department. And in fact, other evidence suggested maybe Billy was a bit lacking in common sense. He not only bit keys in half, he frequently did things like carry a large group of teenagers in the back of his truck …while driving *backwards*…at *60 miles an hour*…on the *highway*. That was a scary 10 minute ride home from school, let me tell you.

The larger point is that it does not take a lot of reflection to see that some people do not seem to have great common sense. This raises the question: Exactly how universal are common sense notions of how to behave? Because Jesus was a moral teacher who focused a lot on practical morality, we'll primarily discuss the moral kind of common sense here. Is Jesus' method of drawing out common sense doomed to fail because there isn't really some kind of shared moral sense to begin with? With respect to moral issues, perhaps there are just too many metaphorical Billy's in the world for the concept of shared simple morality to be meaningful?

Scholars have long debated the universality of human common sense rules. While much evidence exists that there are underlying, shared moral conventions that apply across all cultures,[9,10] it is also true that there is quite a bit of variation. The variation takes several potential forms. In some cases, cultures work from the same larger set of values, but they tend to emphasize different *parts* of those values. For example, while all cultures value the rights of the individual and the good of the group, some cultures are more prone to emphasizing the individual, while others emphasize the group.[11] Thus, there are real cultural differences, but this does not mean that one culture values only the individual while the other values only the group – it means rather that both cultures value both things, yet for cultural reasons they resolve dilemmas involving those sometimes-clashing values differently.

In other cases, cultures show similar emphases in responses to moral dilemmas, but the strength of those emphases differs. Consider a recent study of eight different cultures ranging from big-city United States (e.g., Los Angeles) to rural hunter-gatherers in Africa (e.g., Hadza).[12] In this study, in almost every culture, there was a tendency for persons to view poisoning and physical harm as more morally important than food taboos – and yet, there was variability in the size of that difference. Both in Los Angeles and among the Hadza, for example, food taboos were rated as less important than poisoning; but for the Hadza, the relative difference between food taboos and poisoning was smaller. The study similarly showed that, across all eight cultures, people accounted for the intent of the action in making moral judgments – such that if I believed you ran over a dog by accident, I would be less likely to hold you morally accountable than if I believed you did in on purpose. But some cultures placed greater importance on these mitigating circumstances than others. Thus, oftentimes, the common sense moral principles or values in question are roughly the same across cultures, but they differ in the relative amount of emphasis they place on each value. Basically all the studied cultures recognized common sense notions that not harming others is more important than food taboos, and that people are more morally accountable when they intend to do something than when they don't.

In additional cases, people may share similar moral principles, but apply the principles differently. That application can lead to the appearance of a moral difference when there isn't one. For example, consider people's views of the morally-charged issue of affirmative action. There is certainly a lot of variability in how people view that issue, and one might infer from that variability that it is hard to believe in a universal moral common sense. And yet research[13] reveals a different story: Proponents of affirmative action and opponents of it both base their beliefs on the principle that *the people with the highest degree of merit should get each job*. Proponents and opponents agree on the moral issue – they just disagree on its application in this case. Proponents think affirmative action increases the likelihood of merit-based decisions, while opponents think it decreases that likelihood.

People may share similar moral principles, but apply the principles differently.

Thus, there is a lot of evidence that, underneath apparent variability, there lies some universal similarity. Yet it is unquestionably the case that people sometimes differ on really important moral issues in a real way. While most people at most times in most places would agree that "killing other people for fun is wrong," nonetheless some people think killing is ok in some contexts (e.g., war, self-defense, for religious purposes), while other people do not. Some cultures have endorsed child sacrifice as morally acceptable, and others have endorsed genocide; yet in most cultures, these things are viewed as repugnant. So while, at a larger level, a lot of universal consensus exists on basic morality – most people at most times at most places would consider petting a bunny rabbit to be in a different moral category than torturing the same rabbit – it is also clear that there is a lot of variation.

The Bible actually deals directly with both the universal common elements in our moral common sense *and* the variability. We have seen this already in Chapter 2 when we discussed how the Church solves differences of opinions about moral issues. It is worth noting that while, as we have already discussed at length, Jesus presumes some level of common sense in His audience and tries to draw that sense out, the Bible is also replete with acknowledgments that sometimes, people really do need to be taught moral rules. In the book of Jonah,

God sends Jonah to the city of Nineveh to warn them because the people of the city are doing some bad stuff. And at the end of the book (Jonah 4:11), God says of Nineveh that it contains "one hundred and twenty thousand people who do not know their right hand from their left" – the implication of which is that part of Nineveh's problem was that they simply didn't have moral knowledge. A lot of Jesus' ministry was clearly based on the idea that people needed some moral information that came from outside of them. This is driven home in Mark 6:34: "When Jesus landed and saw a large crowd, he had compassion on them, because they were like sheep without a shepherd. So he began teaching them many things." Jesus also explicitly acknowledges that some people know more than others and thus will be held to different standards. In comparing people who know their master's will with those who do not, Jesus comments in Luke 12:48 that "from everyone who has been given much, much will be demanded; and from the one who has been entrusted with much, much more will be asked." Jesus thus claims not only to call out our common sense but also a Divine authority to teach us right from wrong, whether we feel it in our bones or not.

So I do not think the Bible over-relies on shared common sense notions – in fact, it treats multiple angles of approach to the issue as valid. And yet, importantly, one of those angles that it treats as valid is that people *do* often have a shared common morality.

Does Shared Common Sense Produce Worse Outcomes?

Relatedly, the skeptic might point out that sometimes, common sense methods may simply be ineffective. While it is clearly true that relying on common sense *can* lead to bad outcomes, a large body of emerging research suggests our own common sense intuitions often lead to better practical outcomes than otherwise. Consider the following experiment: Participants are presented with a set of information about four potential roommates. For each roommate, some of the information suggests the roommate will be good, while some suggests the roommate will be bad. However, the information is constructed in such a way that, if the participants process all the information *correctly*, one of the roommates is clearly the best choice based on a good/bad ratio.

Now imagine that some participants, after reading the information, are told to think hard about it for three minutes, while some participants are distracted into thinking about *something else* for those three minutes. Who comes to the right decision? Somewhat surprisingly, perhaps, it is the group that thought about *something else.*[14] Why? Because sometimes, too much hard thinking can interfere with your own intuitive common sense judgments. Indeed, a lot of research suggests that a higher percentage of "right" decisions are often made when people *do not* think too hard about the information, but rather just let their intuitions *percolate* in the background. Other, similar research suggests that using quick-and-easy intuitive heuristics sometimes leads to better outcomes than using a more effort-filled approach to answering questions.[15]

That is not to say that people should avoid thinking! Rather, it is merely to point out the value in shared, often intuitive, common sense mechanisms. Some people may have biases against such shared common sense, but there is no necessary reason to believe that it is *inferior.* All ways of knowing can be useful in their own way.

Christianity relies heavily on direct observation as a means of knowing.

Common Sense Revisited: Christianity Relies on the Power of Observation

Just as rationality has "happened" once in the history of terrestrial life (unlike vision or flight), so science has "happened" only once in the history of humanity (unlike writing or the calendar). And the unique occurrence of science—real science, which does not stop with precise and systematic descriptions of phenomena but goes on to probe their underlying causes—happened in a civilization that was built upon the Church.

Peter van Inwagen,
University of Notre Dame Philosophy Professor[16]

Of course, the attack on Christianity often suggests, not so much that we don't use shared common sense, but rather that we avoid relying on one specific common sense approach: The observation-based scientific method. But this, too, turns out to be false upon closer inspection. Quite the contrary: Christianity relies heavily on direct observation as a means of knowing. Christianity has a large tradition of "look and see" (a fact acknowledged even by a social psychologist such as Brett Pelham in his clever little book about psychological methods).[17] "Taste and *see* that the Lord is good," says the psalmist (Psalm 34:8). "Test me in this and *see*," says the Lord (Malachi 3:10). Even in appealing to his disciples based on the fact that they should grant His authority after being with him for so long, Jesus adds (John 14:11) "or at least believe on the *evidence* of the works themselves." In actual fact, the scriptures are replete with references imploring us to *see* the truth for ourselves, to consider evidence and weigh what we see.

Given a Biblical backstory so infused with practical examples imploring us to rely on our senses, it is hardly surprising that Christians have always assumed God gave us an ability to infer things from our observations of the environment. Indeed, this empirical approach fits with the Christian worldview like a lock and key. We believe God gave us eyes because the things we see really exist; we assume our abilities to discern truth from our world through observation are at least generally functioning well, because we assume God made us to know and understand it.

Indeed, somewhat ironically, the staunchest defenders of the very legs science claims to stand on have historically been Christians. Skeptics have sometimes tried to send people into a sensory blindness; the Church brought the comforting hope that, in fact, we could see. I won't say that science is dependent on Christian epistemology (although a case could be made that this is true)—but I think a softer statement is valid. Surely no one would quibble that Christianity has, whether it was the popular zeitgeist of the time or not, historically defended the human ability to learn through logic and through observation (see: St. Thomas of Aquinas[18]). In doing so – as suggested by prominent Notre Dame philosopher Peter van Inwagen in the above quote – it paved the way for modern science as we know it. As we'll see in Chapter 5, a lot of the empiricists who are credited (by secular and religious historians alike) with creating modern science were Christians. Indeed, the person most often credited with creating the *scientific method* itself, Francis Bacon, was a Christian.

In short, not only does Christianity rely on shared common sense as a means of knowledge in the general sense, it also clearly relies heavily on the observational and empirical approach of the scientific method. We are encouraged to act like scientists ourselves, which is probably one of the reasons we had such a large role in creating *science.*

False Assumption #2:
Science Exclusively Relies on Observation

The intertwining of theory and experiment, inextricably linked by the need to interpret experimental data, does indeed imply that there is an unavoidable degree of circularity involved in scientific reasoning. This means that the nature of science is something more subtle and rationally delicate than simply ineluctable deduction from unquestionable fact.

John Polkinghorne, Cambridge University Physics Professor, from *Quantum Physics and Theology: An Unexpected Kinship*[19]

The Journal Behavioral and Brain Sciences *conducted a survey on the journal review process, the outcome of which gave rise to serious concern among its readers. The discouraging results indicated that scholarship, precision, validity of argument, correctness of results, and originality were by no means the only criteria in deciding the fate of a paper. Among the many other determinants on which an article's acceptance for publication hinges are considerations like whether the author is well known, or at least located at a prestigious institution. In addition, editor-author friendships and old-boy networks play an important role in editorial decision-making.*

George N. Schlesinger, University of North Carolina Philosophy Professor

So the assumption that science has a kind of moratorium on empirical methods of knowing is simply false: Belying the simple story Dennett would have us believe, Christianity rather more complexly uses *all ways* of knowing, and empirical observation is explicitly (and has always been explicitly) a part of that. Equally as important for our purpose, however, is that science is not about empirical observation alone. To hear some people talk, you'd think science had a direct line to truth through observation because it wasn't dependent on anything but direct access to human senses. Few reasonable scientists would say that; but they do often seem to underestimate the importance of the other factors' influence on the practical use of scientific method. And atheists have directly used this argument to claim epistemological superiority over religion, as when atheist Dan Barker says: "The reason the ancient Israelites thought they possessed the source of all knowledge is because it says so in a book that they wrote. As a scientist,

Dawkins knows that knowledge comes not from authority, but from observation."[20]

However, science in reality is dependent on all the ways of knowing, just as dependent in actual fact as Christianity. It is first important to note that the same kinds of common sense judgments we discussed for moral and religious instincts apply in the same way to the scientific method. To take an example from my own field, there is no way to conclusively determine whether or not *extraversion* is really measured by *the amount of talking at a dinner party*, except that talking a lot at dinner intuitively *seems like* extraversion. It appears to our minds as a self-evident relationship based on common sense. Or consider another example closer to my own line of research: I was recently involved in a symposium for the journal *Political Psychology* where experts on cognitive complexity came together to discuss the best method of scoring it via computer. Symposium members disagreed on a lot of things—but the one thing we *did* agree on is that the ultimate standard for success in measurement was whether or not humans would agree with the computer that a particular passage was complex.[21] This means that at some fundamental level, we agreed that the only way we could ultimately judge the complexity of a passage was that it *seemed* complex—that is, if common sense suggested it was complex. Scientists are humans, too, and ultimately our human standards of judgment at almost every level are based in large part upon common intuitions.

Equally as importantly, science uses appeals to authority in rabid abundance everywhere. Consider as one example that we are constantly citing other people in our work. Why? We did not run the studies we cite or personally investigate most of the conclusions drawn – we simply rely on the authority of the people we read. In fact, in my own field, most psychologists don't directly run the studies they report as their own—they trust the authority of the research assistants who ran the study. No progress could be made in science without this reliance on authority. If I did not trust researchers that the basic facts they reported were generally accurate, then I would be unable to build in any way upon that work. Every research study would be like starting over.

Further, scientists readily cite researchers at Harvard more than researchers at McClennan Community College. Why? Is it because they have personally read the relevant research reports at each university and determined, in each case, that the McClennan report is inferior?

No. They do so because of authority: They simply trust Harvard as an authority and do not trust McClennan. I'm not arguing this is a bad (or good) thing—only that it is not a unique thing to my religion. It is a universal part of the human experience to trust expert authority, both in science and religion and everywhere. The key thing is not "whether" but "which": You *will* trust authority, but you must decide which ones to trust. After all, Jesus himself warned us to choose our authority figures wisely and with caution (Matthew 7:15).

It is a universal part of the human experience to trust expert authority, both in science and religion and everywhere.

False Assumption #3: Observation Is Better than Other Ways of Knowing

Among those who are under a king, there are differences. Some experience his rule in a more mystic, hidden, and divine way. However, others experience it in a less perfect fashion. Some are led by reason, apart from all agencies of sense. They have beheld the incorporeal things (the things Paul speaks of as "invisible" and "not seen").

Origen[22]

I think people often lazily imagine that the power of observation which underlies the scientific method is philosophically better than other ways of knowing. But closer scrutiny shows at once that this is not so. In fact, all ways of knowing require faith in something that ultimately cannot be tested: Authority in the competence of the source, logic in the power of human reason, observation in the power of human inference. The idea that trusting our power to infer truth from observations is somehow more worthy may exist in your mind: But it almost certainly exists because you have been taught so by others, not because it is self-evident. There is no reason I should (necessarily) trust my senses when I see a ghost (an empirical observation) as opposed to trusting my mother who assures me ghosts don't exist (an authority figure). The difficulty is the same in either case: I either rely on my power of inferring the nature of reality from my senses (which we know can go wrong) or on other people's ability to know reality (which we know can go wrong).

This isn't merely a semantic game. My specialty area of social psychology has been almost entirely devoted over the last thirty years to demonstrating the many ways our observational inference processes go wrong. Take one example from literature about stereotyping: We can see the exact same behaviors exhibited by (say) a black man and a white man, or a man and a woman, and come to totally different conclusions as to what the behavior means. The black man was behaving aggressively; the white man was playing.[23] The woman was behaving as a mean-spirited jerk; the man was behaving assertively. Nothing about the *reality* of the behaviors was different: But the interpretations differed wildly. This is just one example picked at random—I could name a hundred. Everything we know about human processing suggests we *construct* reality from the very first moments of processing—we don't just represent it, we interpret it, and often those interpretations are wrong. And this is what pure empiricists who worship the power of observation-only evidence would have us base our hope on? On the human ability to infer through observation?

Everything we know about human processing suggests we *construct* reality from the very first moments of processing—we don't just represent it, we interpret it, and often those interpretations are wrong.

Of course, I am not trying to send the reader into a well of skepticism: Often our observational inference processes seem right. I only mention it to say it isn't just a trick about ghosts to point out that observation itself teaches us our observation mechanism may not always work so well (just as reason itself teaches reasonable skepticism of reason, and authority figures like Jesus often tell us to be wary of authority). Thus we can't just assume with blind faith that it always works. So it is not necessarily on any better ground than the other ways of knowing.

On the flip side, this over-belief in observation is also fueled by a silly under-belief in authority. The vast majority of what you and I know we learned from authority. Does that make it wrong? Of course not. Consider the statement "George Washington was the first president of the U.S." I strongly suspect that, although you believe in that uncontroversial statement, you did not personally witness it. In fact, I seriously doubt you have even seen actual reports of the historical research. No, you likely just believed your first-grade history teacher, who in turn believed her college professor, who in turn believed some historian, who in turn believed what someone wrote in a historical document (believed on the authority of an expert) to be legitimate. But does all of that chain of authority make the fact itself wrong? Of course not. The *method* through which one learns something does not dictate its truth or falsehood. It is similarly possible, though unlikely, that you learned 2 + 2 = 4 by discovering the truth of mathematics through empirical trial-and-error. But it is more probable that you learned it from your first-grade teacher. Either way, whether discovered through empirical trial or through authority, it is still *true*.

Thus, while I am a huge fan of empirical methods myself, I think it is important to neither over-value what observation can do, nor under-value what other ways of learning can do.

The *method* through which one learns something does not dictate its truth or falsehood.

An Epistemological Hypocrisy Challenged

So what are we to make, then, of Dennett's attack on religion? Just this: It is based on a too-simple view of how we actually learn; it is a kind of epistemological hypocrisy. It ignores the full picture of knowledge that Dennett himself must be committed to—even in order to maintain his own views. This can be seen in his arguments' required assumptions (all false) that Christianity does not rely on shared common sense (it does), that science only relies on observation (it doesn't), and that observation is obviously a superior way of knowing (it isn't).

The purpose of this chapter is simply to point out that for *anyone* to fully know *anything*—or anything *big*—they are likely going to use both authority and observation (and every kind of method in between). It can't be helped. And Christianity acknowledges this fact. Christians love empiricism and observational learning; yet we not only *use* the other forms of knowing (as all people do), but we also *acknowledge* that these other forms of learning, too, are worthy of consideration. And in applying this more complex view of knowledge – in explicitly using all the ways of knowing in their proper place – we help the human machine run well.

CHAPTER FOUR

BOUNDARIES MEET FREEDOM: THE PSYCHOLOGY OF HAPPINESS

The more you abandon to God the care of all temporal things, the more He will take care to provide for all your wants.
St. Jean Baptiste de la Salle[1]

He who desires nothing but God is rich and happy.
St. Alphonsus Liguori[2]

Have you ever had a day where everyone *on earth* irritated you? Where no matter *what* they did, it made you angry?

I remember having a day like that once. I was driving to work and complaining out loud about *everything*. I was saying hard-to-comprehend and super-whiny things like: "Look at that kid…*walking*…on the SIDEWALK! What *is* this modern generation coming to? Flippin' generation X. Bunch o' sidewalk-walking jerks." But that wasn't enough: "And look at *that* idiot…pulling into McDonald's…eating BREAKFAST! The nerve. I didn't want to have to see *that*. Breakfast is sooooo stupid."

Looking back, I honestly have no idea what made me upset that day. It obviously had something to do with me and not with the people walking *on the designated place for walking* or eating breakfast at *normal breakfast-eating times*. On the flipside, there have been plenty of days where I've just been inexplicably happy and I could not tell you why. I remember once feeling such extreme happiness that I thought *this must be the Holy Spirit moving! I'm finally feeling the love of God!* And then I looked down at the litany of empty coffee cups in front of me…and considered the sobering alternative that I may have *just had one too many espressos*. Who knows? This is why we have expressions like "I must have gotten up on the wrong side of the bed this morning" and "I feel unspeakable joy" – we often have no earthly idea where our emotions come from.

In this chapter, I aim to illustrate how Christianity makes people happy because it appropriately helps us navigate the complexity of the human

We often have no earthly idea where our emotions come from.

machine. It makes us emotionally *run right.* I know that this task will not be easy, because the causes of our happiness are both complicated and hard to identify. Given this difficulty, it is perhaps unsurprising that the relationship between religion and happiness has been the subject of some controversy.

Let's start our question at home by pondering that sample of one I generally consider the most persuasive: Myself.

Does Religion Make People Happy?

You may have surmised by now that I am religious. And I have been described as an incredibly happy person. However, those who describe me this way don't know me very well. Anyone who actually *knows* me knows that I am an angsty, up-and-down emotional roller coaster of a person who sometimes has a hard time getting up in the morning. I have been known to cry…frequently…while watching such sappy and touchy-feely programs as *Godzilla versus Mothra* and *The Incredible Hulk* and episodes of the rough-and-tumble murder-solving show *NCIS*. And I don't mean I get emotional at the actual *sad parts* of NCIS – though that's true, too – I mean I cry at the parts where hipster Tony Dinozzo is making seemingly-insensitive jokes about the murdered victim's bad hairstyle. (You have to admit, a mullet *is* a kind of tragedy.)

So you might think this admission is a bad opening to a chapter trying to convince you that Christianity makes the human machine run well. And you'd be partially right about that. But actually, taken in total, my life nonetheless makes the point of this chapter beautifully. There are a *lot* of things that contribute to why you might feel happy or unhappy at a given point in time. Few people are happy when they have a severe migraine. Few people are unhappy in the moment after they take heroin. Well and good. But the point of this chapter is that there is a tendency for some things to lead people to be happy and content overall, whereas other things tend to make people happy in some short-term sense – but that isn't the general direction they lead in the long-term.

And when I turn to myself, this is what I find, without doubt and without hesitation: Following Jesus has unquestionably made me *happier.* Yes, I am naturally an angsty person whose entire day was once ruined by having tissues that were too rough on my nose (don't laugh, that can be really sensitive) – but that's how I would be in any world no matter what I believed. The real question for comparison is: What was I like when I did *not* follow Christ? And I remember that all too well. I was a horrible, pitiful, miserable shell of a man; depressed; without life and without hope. And now I am not: I am still angsty, sure, but I have hope, I have thankfulness, I feel blessed, I feel peace, I feel goodness. These things are not perfectly formed in me – yet – but they are there, and they were not there in any great or consistent measure without Jesus in my life (or, in common parlance, without Christianity). I grew up fearing the thunderstorm; it was Jesus who taught me to dance in the rain.

And evidence suggests it is not just me. The subject of religion and happiness is controversial, but overall, it is fair to say that at least some evidence suggests that religious people the world over are happier than non-religious people. For example, one international survey showed that holding religious beliefs was associated with self-reported happiness both across and within countries.[3,4] In our own data, we have also consistently found that across the U.S., religious people (primarily Christians) are happier. Thus, there are good reasons to believe that religious people generally, and Christians specifically, are a pretty happy lot.

I grew up fearing the thunderstorm;
it was Jesus who taught me to dance in the rain.

What Atheists Say

Atheists themselves seem to disagree on whether religious people are genuinely happier. There have been roughly two views: One claims religion makes people unhappy and unhealthy; and one admits religion has positive benefits but thinks those benefits are like a crutch we need to grow out of. We'll discuss each of these briefly before getting to the larger point of the chapter – which is relevant to both attacks.

Some Atheists Claim Religion Does Not Make People Happy

Some atheists think religion is simply unnecessary for happiness, such as famous religion critic, Christopher Hitchens, (in his book *god is Not Great*):

God is not necessary for someone to find fulfilment in contemplation or social activity.[5]

Some atheists go further, clearly using psychological arguments about how religion ruins happiness – they think religion actually holds people back from being happy, healthy, normal people because it is too restrictive. Consider perhaps the most famous atheist of the past century, Bertrand Russell, who said in his book *Why I am Not a Christian*:

There are a great many ways in which, at the present moment, the church, by its insistence upon what it chooses to call morality, inflicts upon all sorts of people undeserved and unnecessary suffering.[6]

More recently, atheist Victor J. Stenger wrote in his book *God and the Folly of Faith*:

Any health benefits of religious practice are problematical…And what about the negative impact that religion has on health?[7]

In other words, some atheists explicitly use as an argument against Christianity the practical claim that it stands opposed to happiness and health. As we shall see, there is ample reason to doubt this assertion.

Some Atheists Claim Religion is a Spell to Be Broken or a Crutch to Leave Behind

On the other hand, plenty of atheists do seem to think religion makes people happier. Consider these powerful words from famous atheist philosopher Daniel Dennett:

Some people had endured hardships that I could not readily imagine myself surviving, and some had found in their religion the strength to make, and hold fast to, decisions that were nothing short of heroic.[8]

Yet, Dennett thinks that humanity should still leave religion behind, and indeed considers it like a spell that needs to be broken (as evidenced by the title of his book on religion called "Breaking the Spell").

Going even further, some atheists respond to the fact that religion makes people happy with a kind of condescending derision: The happiness it produces is almost grounds for rejecting it as a comfortable illusion. These words from talk show host Dick Cavett about his religious background typify that point of view:

It would be wonderful to believe…it would make life easier, it would explain everything, it would give meaning…but something about knowing it could instantly make me happier makes it somehow unworthy of having.[9]

Similarly, famous Russian author Fyodor Dostoyevsky – who is one of my personal favorite writers – said of religious people:

Peacefully they will die…and beyond the grave they will find nothing but death. But we shall keep the secret, and for their happiness we shall allure them with the reward of heaven and eternity.[10]

Clarence Darrow, the famous American lawyer at the Scopes trial that evaluated the use of evolution in schools, summed it up by saying:

Some of you say religion makes people happy. So does laughing gas.[11]

One way to characterize the commonly-expressed view is to say that a lot of people think Christianity is a kind of artificial crutch that props people up. It may make people happy sometimes; but that happiness is temporary and delusional, and we would be better off to learn to be happy on our own two solid feet.

Christian Response

In the present chapter, we approach this issue by considering the psychological underpinnings of long-term happiness and compare that to what Christianity teaches. And we will see that, for this one skeptic at least, the Christian map clearly fits the emerging psychological picture of the complicated happiness landscape. Far from being an artificial crutch that leads to short-term delusions and long-term pain, Christianity in fact teaches things that are far more likely to produce long-term happiness than otherwise.

Christians are, in my experience, happy people. I think the reason we are happy is because Christianity meets deep-seated needs in human psychology. We will discuss some of those in more depth in the next chapter. In this chapter, however, I'll explore a practical tension that Christianity helps resolve: The tension between the free expression of passions and boundaries. Although providing boundaries is not a uniquely Christian approach, the issue is nonetheless one of the reasons Christianity is often most attacked – and the critics are wrong.

Free Passions versus Common Sense Boundaries: The Heart and the Mind

Almost everyone likes the freedom to do what they want. Research repeatedly shows that people react quite negatively when they feel their freedom taken away and often work to re-establish their right to choose[12,13,14] To illustrate: Imagine your favorite kind of peanut butter. Now imagine that I told you that, for the rest of your life, you *had* to eat nothing but *that* kind of peanut butter. Would you be happy? After all, it's your favorite, right?

Odds are, the answer is *no,* you would not be happy. In fact, it's more likely that you'd go out and buy a different kind of peanut butter (which you would curiously suddenly like "better") just to show you won't be told what to do. It is for this reason that the worst thing any persuader can do to an audience she hopes to persuade is to *tell them she is trying to manipulate them.*[15] People don't want to be persuaded by manipulation – they want to *choose* what they want. We want our passions to be passions, freely expressed and unregulated by external boundaries.

This is hardly surprising from a Christian point of view: The Bible teaches we were made for freedom. In the Garden of Eden, Adam and Eve were given only *one* rule – they were literally allowed to do anything else, to eat of any tree, go anywhere they wanted – freedom (Genesis 2:15-17). While we don't know for sure what living in the Garden of Eden was like, the Bible clearly teaches that, at least with respect to their own desires for fruit, their behavior was free to be largely dictated by their own passions. Paul echoes the importance of freedom in the New Testament when he says "It is for freedom that Christ has made you free" (Galatians 5:1).

On the other hand, maybe less obviously but no less pervasively, we also like rules and order. You may want freedom to choose your own peanut butter; but you don't want your neighbor to have freedom to walk into your house and steal *your* peanut butter.[16,17] And although psychologically appealing, the free rein of passions can also be psychologically paralyzing. Sometimes, we actually would be happier if someone else just picked the peanut butter for us – that is, if someone else dictated the boundary.[18]

So both a desire to let our passions run free and a desire for restrictions seem built into us. Yet these things are often in conflict with each other – how can we be free if we are restricted?

So both a desire to let our passions run free and a desire for restrictions seem built into us.

Borrowing from another common metaphor, we sometimes have a conflict between our heart and our head. Proverbs 13:12 says: "Hope deferred makes the heart sick, but a longing fulfilled is a tree of life." We will not be whole until our passions are fulfilled. And yet, we cannot just live our lives in submission to our passions in a senseless fashion, as it says in 1 Thessalonians 4:4-6: "Each of you should learn to control your own body in a way that is holy and honorable, not in passionate lust like the pagans, who do not know God; and that in this matter no one should wrong or take advantage of a brother or sister."

Christianity provides numerous roadmaps for helping us navigate the set of complex tensions involved in common sense boundaries and our free passions. We will start at the end that is probably the least popular – the value of boundaries.

The Psychological Value of Common Sense Boundaries

The Christian ideal has not been tried and found wanting.
It has been found difficult; and left untried.
G. K. Chesterton[19]

Chesterton's claim is hyperbolic, perhaps; but it contains a grain of truth. Often we do not experience the joys of life because they require stuff that, on the surface, does not seem like joy. The route to happiness is often through a path that seems like unhappiness; and we don't want any of that. So we never set out on the journey at all.

When I was in college, I had this great idea to make chocolate chip cookies without a recipe book. I felt like an expert at this sort of thing because I once watched part of a cooking show with my grandmother. Granted, I was almost certainly wearing headphones and listening to *Journey* during the show—and that particular episode might have been about making clam chowder—but really, how hard could it be? I was, after all, a college student, and college students are *smart people.*

So I got some flour, butter, eggs, sugar, and chocolate chips and dumped them into a big bowl. I had a hard time getting the consistency right—first it seemed too runny (so I added more flour) and then it seemed too thick (more eggs and butter) and then too runny (more flour). And gradually that lump of cookie batter kept growing and growing until it became a sixteen-pound bowling ball o' chocolate-chippy glory.

Finally, to my delight, the batter looked and tasted quite like real cookie dough, and I proudly put a batch of cookies into the oven to bake. When they came out, they looked...well, they looked like... *liquid.* Rather than bake and rise, my cookie batter had...melted. I had basically made a really gross-looking cookie dough soup. (A soup that, coincidentally, looked *curiously like clam chowder.* But I digress.)

Now you might think I'd have thrown the whole batch of clam chowder cookie batter out and started over. If so, you clearly don't remotely understand the mind of a 20-year-old college student who lives off 25-cent mac-and-cheese and is always hungry. No, rather than throw it out, I instead followed this logical train of thought: (a) I can't make cookies with that cookie batter, (b) I don't like melted cookie dough soup, (c) I think my odds of ever making *real, normal-looking* cookies with another attempt are pretty low, (d) raw cookie batter tastes better than baked cookies anyway, (e) *my* raw cookie batter tasted like real cookie dough as long as you didn't actually try to cook it, and (f) that cookie batter will go bad in a matter of hours. The net result of that chain of reasoning was that I decided to eat the *whole giant mass* of uncooked cookie dough in about 20 minutes.

And let me tell you two things about that. First, it tasted really, really good. I mean, that was an absolutely epic 20 minutes of eating. Second, the 20 minutes *after that* were pretty awful. It became quickly apparent that this was a really, *really* horrible idea and I got terribly sick. *Do not eat a giant bowl of cookie batter in 20 minutes, kids. That's a free tip.*

Now, the point of the story is this. Despite being a hungry college student apparently destined to do stupid things for pleasure, I actually knew—somewhere deep inside of me—that eating a sixteen-pound-bowling-ball-o-raw-clam-chowder-cookie-dough *in one sitting* was probably not the *best* idea I'd ever had. Some common sense buried within my mind tried to revolt against the idea, but I pushed it down, ignored it, and focused on the one thing in front of me: The pleasure of eating that cookie dough. And that was stupid.

We Tend To Eschew Boundaries

I am Mastos, god of sensible spending.
No one has listened to me for the last thirty years.
From the YouTube *Studio C* skit, *Pantheon of the Gods.*

This cookie dough story is a parable of human life. Most people I know have this kind of deep common sense imbedded in them, and yet all those same people seem to ignore it a lot of the time. As suggested by Studio C's fake sensible spending god, *Mastos*, in the above quote—our culture clearly has come to increasingly ignore our sensible, rule-setting side in favor of our passionate, ignore-the-rules side.

Will that work? I do not think so. One of the lessons of Christianity is that ultimate happiness requires boundaries; it requires restricting oneself. If we would set sail through those turbulent waters, we will find the metaphorical Treasure

Our culture clearly has come to increasingly ignore our sensible, rule-setting side in favor of our passionate, ignore-the-rules side.

Island on the other side. We are told to die to ourselves; to put boundaries on ourselves and follow rules; to focus on other people first, and in return we will get Divine joy. We are told Christ Himself endured the cross for the joy that awaited Him on the other side (Hebrews 12:2). Joy and sacrifice are twins; freedom and boundaries are partners; righteousness and peace kiss each other.

Even though we have the common sense to see it when presented with it, our "everything now" American minds are growing increasingly distant from this idea. But it is true nonetheless that the path to true joy runs directly through self-sacrifice and setting boundaries on our own ego.

Is Self-Control Good or Bad for People?: The Value of Listening to Our Own Common Sense Boundaries

Research suggests this value isn't just limited to me. In the 1980s and 1990s, the self-esteem movement swept the country. This movement fundamentally claimed that the primary problem with people is that they don't feel good about themselves, and that making them feel good about themselves should be priority number one. This wasn't just a short-term pop psychology fad. It produced many governmental social initiatives targeted to improve self-esteem in schools (among other things).[20] It also has led to the increasingly growing cultural idea that things previously described as "sinful" are actually good for you, because they make you feel good about yourself (as evidenced by the recent book title *The Science of Sin: The Psychology of the Seven Deadlies and Why They Are So Good For You*)[21].

Part of this social cultural milieu resulted from the influence of psychology. Indeed, for a long, long time in the field of psychology, one of the primary guiding beliefs among researchers was that self-esteem – or holding yourself in high positive regard – was the most important predictor of a happy life.[22] This suggests that the primary way to a happy life was to simply make people feel good about themselves. And that was the party line in my field for quite a while.

But watch what happened next. In what might be described as one of the biggest "oops, sorry about that!" moments in research history, many psychologists have begun to wildly backtrack on these assertions.[23] Roy Baumeister, who is perhaps the most famous social psychologist in the world – he's been on Oprah and 20/20, for crying out loud! – started out as a self-esteem researcher.[24] But he decided that the field had been wrong about self-esteem. So what makes people happy, according to Baumeister? I'll quote his own words on 20/20:

> *If we're concerned about raising children to be successful and healthy and happy, forget about self-esteem. Concentrate on self-control. Studies show that self-control does predict success in life over a very long time.*

It is the ability to resist temptations of things we know are bad for us that ultimately makes us happy.

In other words, it is the ability to resist temptations of things we know are bad for us that ultimately makes us happy.[25] Boundaries are necessary for a good life. Our nation does not have a self-esteem problem; we have an impulse control problem. We have a problem following our *own* common sense which tells us boundaries are good for us. Happy people – people most satisfied with their lives – know how to control their impulses towards sin. They know how to *discipline themselves;* how to *resist temptation.*

Everyone knows sin has short-term positive benefits, but that doesn't mean it's going to make you happy long-term. Those things that make you happy at the moment won't necessarily lead to the happiest life. Drugs make most people happy temporarily; but when you use drugs, you are trading in your long-term happiness for short-term bursts of pleasure. Well, a *lot* of sin is like that – feels good now, but feels crummy in the big picture of my life. Contrary to the general zeitgeist suggesting that sin will make you happy, research suggests that happy people are actually those that can *resist* the 10th cookie (gluttony) and *avoid* the impulse for sex outside of marriage (lust). Resisting the temptation to give in to sin will often have short-term negative consequences, sure, but long-term, it is more likely to make you satisfied with your life than not.

Our nation does not have a self-esteem problem; we have an impulse control problem.

The Glory of Free Desire: Come to the Joy-Filled Feast

"Please don't eat raw cookie dough." Why, Pillsbury? Worried I might be happy for FIVE [expletive deleted] MINUTES? #christmas #drunk #crying.
Tweet from Patton Oswalt.

Cookie dough might make you sick. Eating it raw might be condemned by the Pillsbury company. But there is no denying that cookie dough *is* freakishly awesome. If you do not see *that*—if you do not believe eating a bowl of raw cookie dough is a sublime experience that makes you want to quit your job and become a cookie-dough-tester for a living—then you are not the discerning reader I take you for, and please go immediately hand this book to a normal human being who can appreciate good food experiences.[xii]

In fact, if you are like me, you might respond to the appeal to common sense boundaries in the previous section a little like this:

OK, fine, I grant that sometimes we don't listen to our common sense when we should. Well and good. I grant that Jesus teaches us that, but so does Confucius and Bill Maher and Richard Dawkins. But surely there is more to life than just common sense? I mean, I get that you should not eat 16 pounds of cookie dough, but—well, cookie dough is still awesome! In some way, cookie dough is more important to me than common sense rules about not eating it. So if Christianity just means listening to common sense, it is pretty poor fare. If I had to choose, I'd choose cookie dough—it may make me sick sometimes, but it's still a glorious 20 minutes!

I feel like that sometimes, too. I not only find inside of me something that says that eating too much cookie dough is bad, I also find something inside of me that says eating cookie dough *at all* is wonderfully good. In fact, part of me wants to revolt against my common sense. I can resonate with G.K. Chesterton when he said (in his amazing book *Orthodoxy*) this about common sense:

[xii] Some people have claimed I have a bias in favor of cookie dough. It is true that upon discovering a shop in Bend, Oregon that served giant bowls of raw cookie dough (in its pure form, as God meant it to be eaten – unsullied by unnecessary idiocies such as *ice cream*), I was completely giddy with delight. But the rumor that I "squealed like a little girl and fainted" is a reckless exaggeration.

> *We have all forgotten what we really are. All that we call common sense and rationality and practicality and positivism only means that for certain dead levels of our life we forget that we have forgotten. All that we call spirit and art and ecstasy only means that for one awful moment we remember that we forget.*[26]

Humans are passionate beings who love to feel the freedom of pleasure. There is infinitely more to life than simply acknowledging our deeper common sense—more to life than merely engaging in "sound and prudent judgment." And for any theory to help put the human machine right, it has to understand and acknowledge this fact. If it didn't—if that theory somehow said passion and desire was bad through and through—I would refuse to believe it.

There is infinitely more to life than simply acknowledging our deeper common sense—more to life than merely engaging in "sound and prudent judgment."

How are we do deal with the intensities of human desire? Some people think they are pretty bad through and through. Famous skeptic and philosopher Michel de Montaigne once said "to understand via the heart is *not* to understand." You see, Montaigne did not like human passions. He thought of marriage as a horrid necessity to populate the species, not as a glorious romantic enterprise. He feared the power of basic human emotions interfered with real life. He would have *hated* cookie dough.

Jesus was not like that. He didn't try to convince us that real life meant completely setting aside, for all time, human passions. He called us to pay attention to our deeper common sense, but he didn't dismiss our normal passions as bad. Jesus wasn't opposed to intense passion or pleasure or desire.

Quite the contrary. Jesus actually *appealed* to our passions. Consider that—after imploring His disciples to keep His commands—Jesus didn't say, "I have told you this so your *self-control* may be complete." He didn't say, "I have told you this so your *sacrificial attitudes* may be complete." He didn't say, "I have told you this so your *mind* may be complete." All those things are true, but it is an often-overlooked fact that what Jesus actually *said* was, "I have told you this that your *joy* may be complete" (John 15:11).

Jesus talked of common sense and moral rules and self-control, yes, but He also talked of endless joy (John 15:11) and feasting (Luke 13:29) and mansions in Heaven (John 14:2-3) and living life to the fullest (John 10:10). He shamelessly appealed to people's desire for food and shelter and happiness. And this emphasis on enjoyment is spread throughout the Bible. As it says in 1 Timothy 6:17, God "gives us richly all things to *enjoy*."

When Boundaries *Meet* Passion: The Marriage of the Heart and the Head

A metaphorical 30,000-foot aerial view of the Bible reveals both the prudent common sense side of human nature *and* our passionate side. Consider a simple linguistic analysis. The Bible uses a word that's been translated "heart" 725 times, but it also uses a word translated "mind" 163 times. Quite astonishingly, these two words—*heart* and *mind*—appear together *in the same verse* 27 times. In three of these places, Jesus identifies Old Testament law's primary moral injunction (Matthew 22:37; Mark 12:30, Luke 10:27). In other words, the Bible doesn't just discuss the heart and the head, it explicitly puts them together.

Of course, the fact that heart and mind appear together is just a superficial linguistic analysis; most of those references do not do any heavy lifting toward the reconciliation of the heart and the head. But it is representative of the Christian approach to common sense boundaries and passion. Christianity teaches that people can go wrong by failing to deal with either side of this complex psychological dilemma. I have probably spent more time in this chapter trying to convince you we need to acknowledge our common sense because it seems to me and to lots of other people that we are increasingly prone to lose our way by exchanging our own and other people's possible long-term joy for our own certain short-term self-interest.

But, if common sense rules are *all* we have, Christ will call us out of our purely sensible complacency. Indeed, in ages where there was too much focus on pleasure-reducing discipline, Christianity has often called people to focus on joy and passion.

Consider a brief historical example. My guess is you've never heard of Manichaeism. But for quite a while back in the third through seventh centuries, it was one of the most popular religions in the whole world. I do not want to do injustice to Manichaeism, which was very complex—but it had an ascetic ideology that claimed there was something wrong with material things and pleasure. It may surprise you to know that Christianity largely fought this ideology. In fact, one of the most famous Christian apologists of all time, St. Augustine, converted to Manichaeism but subsequently renounced it. Here is what he said about it in *Confessions*:

> *Insensibly and little by little, I was led on to such follies as to believe that a fig tree wept when it was plucked and that the sap of the mother tree was tears…And, wretch that I was, I believed that more mercy was to be shown to the fruits of the earth than unto men, for whom these fruits were created. For, if a hungry man—who was not a Manichean—should beg for any food, the morsel that we gave to him would seem condemned, as it were, to capital punishment.*[27]

In other words, Augustine reacted negatively to the idea that people should not enjoy the fruits for what they are. Ultimately, in Christianity, he found a belief system that met both sides of the pleasure/boundaries equation.

I've found this, too. I know that at some point after I had given my life to Christ, I went through a phase where I become obsessed by the "rules." Little else mattered to me. I never quite understood the Biblical teachings which called us out of prudence-bound rules and into the Spirit. So I ignored them. I became bound by rules and rules and more rules until I was almost more miserable than I was when I was a horrible sinner. In fact, people who knew me during both phases said that I was *more* miserable to be around during my rule-bound phase than in my reckless sinning phase. And what called me out of that horrible nightmare of focus on rules?

It was Jesus' own words in the New Testament. One day, I read these words from Jesus (John 10:9-10): "I am the gate; whoever enters through me will be saved. They will come in and go out, and find pasture. The thief comes only to steal and kill and destroy; I have come that they may have life, and have it to the full."

Those words hit me like a lightning bolt because my life did not feel *full* at all. It did not feel like the feast or the mansion or the joy-filled ride Jesus describes. It did not feel like going through a gate into a green pasture—it felt like a giant fence I had erected to protect a single dying weed. Jesus's words shocked me into seeking the thing He put in front of me, the thing He said He offered. And that journey did not lead me to abandon my common sense—any more than the Bible teaches following the Spirit means abandoning the Ten Commandments—but rather, it taught me how to find life and joy and happiness *within* prudence. They are not mutually exclusive. In the words of the psalmist, righteousness and peace kiss each other.

So we need both heart *and* the head. We need to put them together in the right amounts. If you can build a transmission but cannot build a gas tank, your car will not run. If you can build a gas tank but have no transmission, your car will not run. We need both desire and common sense, working together, to function.

In the next couple of sections, we discuss specifically how common sense rules, far from destroying passion, actually preserve it in its best and purest form.

Common Sense Rules Produce Happiness

The only way to get rid of a temptation is to yield to it. Resist it, and your soul grows sick with longing for the things it has forbidden to itself.
Oscar Wilde, in *The Picture of Dorian Gray*[28]

When I read about the evils of drinking, I gave up reading.
Henny Youngman[29]

[The church] is in its major part an opponent of all progress and of improvement in all the ways that diminish suffering in the world, because it has chosen to label as morality a certain narrow set of rules of conduct which have nothing to do with human happiness.
Bertrand Russell, in *Why I am Not a Christian*[30]

The term "boundaries" is not often associated with words like "fun" or "happiness," and yet we just reviewed evidence that suggests it *should* be. And you may wonder: What is going on here? Why are self-controlled boundaries so important for happiness?

I think there are several related reasons. The first is probably the most straightforward: People cannot have a lot of fun – at least, not for very long – when they do not have boundaries. "Boundaries *discourage* fun, because then we can't do exactly what we want!" says the anti-religious skeptic. The Christian replies: "Boundaries *encourage* fun, because we know what *not* to do so we won't hurt ourselves – and therefore we can gleefully and playfully do anything else!" As G.K. Chesterton said,

> "Catholic doctrine and discipline may be walls; but they are the walls of a playground. We might fancy some children playing on the flat grassy top of some tall island in the sea. So long as there was a wall round the cliff's edge they could fling themselves into every frantic game and make the place the noisiest of nurseries. But the walls were knocked down, leaving the naked peril of the precipice. They did not fall over, but when their friends returned to them they were all huddled in terror in the center of the island; and their song had ceased."[31]

Consider the famous parable of the prodigal son Jesus tells in the book of Luke (Chapter 15). In that parable, the son thought he would have more fun by leaving the boundaries of his father's house. And for a while, he did. But eventually, he ended up wasting his money, taken advantage of by so-called friends, and so destitute he found himself eating the food of pigs. Life without boundaries is like that – it starts out with a bang and ends with fighting pigs for your next meal. The unbridled pursuit of passion always cheats us in the end, and the passion itself fizzles into nothing. But note this: When the son came to his senses and went home, he didn't go home to a horrible prison. He went home to a *party*. His father threw him a feast to *celebrate with his friends*. The boundaries of the father's house weren't to keep fun out – they were to keep fun *in*. They were to keep the eternal party eternal. They were for the son's enjoyment, because the father knows that the end result otherwise will involve a lot of pig food.

> The boundaries of the father's house weren't to keep fun out – they were to keep fun *in*.

Consider too the example of drinking alcohol. Christianity does not teach that drinking alcohol is bad. But it does teach restraint and reasonable boundaries (for example, in Ephesians 5:18). And about those boundaries, sometimes I have heard people say things like "Christians don't have any fun because we won't let loose with alcohol."

But it is practically common sense to see that Christianity is right and the skeptics are wrong. If a person allows themselves to drink as much as they "want," they will generally drink too much; they increase their odds of becoming a drunkard. And the nearly universal testimony of humanity is that being a drunkard is not fun. Try an experiment. Walk into a group of people and tell them "I'm thinking of becoming an adventure tour guide in the Rocky Mountains!" You will get all kinds of reactions; but a certain subset of people will react like this: "That sounds fun! Wow! How exciting!" Now, with a different group of people, walk in and tell them "I'm thinking of becoming a drunkard!" You may get different kinds of reactions; but one reaction I guarantee you that you will *not* get is this: "That sounds fun! Wow! How exciting!" You see, almost nobody – including drunkards – considers a *life* of drunkenness *fun* and *full of happiness.*

The natural drift of humans, if we do what we want in the immediate present all the time, is to drink more than we should. But drinking more than we should isn't fun; no one thinks it creates a fun life. If we want to even enjoy alcohol, then, we require some boundaries. It is a behavioral paradox: The undisciplined pursuit of fun at each moment will not lead to a fun life. The truly fun life requires boundaries – boundaries that are set and followed. Within those boundaries, people can play with abandon and know they can play with the same abandon – and the same amount of fun – tomorrow. Without those boundaries, people may have "fun" at the moment, but the natural tendency is for that fun to get less and less until a lifestyle of misery results. That is one of the many reasons why I think, on average, Christians have much more fun than anybody – our fun is an abandonment, but an abandonment with security. And, like all truly good and eternal things, it does not diminish over time. In the words of the Psalmist (Psalms 16:11): "You make known to me the path of life; you will fill me with joy in your presence, with eternal pleasures at your right hand."[xiii]

[xiii] Of course, disputes exist about exactly *what* rules should be applied. We dealt with some of the issues surrounding disputes over rules in Chapters 2 and 3; however, in this chapter, I intentionally avoid hotly disputed areas – both areas that Christians debate with each other *and* areas that Christians debate with the secular culture at large. The primary point of this chapter is navigating the general tension between rules and passion, and not on explicitly arguing for a particular set of Christian rules. It is the larger psychological approach that I want readers to see. However, it is worth noting that Christians do sometimes have disputes with secular culture about which rules to apply, and I do not intend to minimize that. It is worth reminding the reader in this regard of evidence – some

Lasting Happiness Will Not Be Artificial

The fact that a believer is happier than a sceptic is no more to the point than the fact that a drunken man is happier than a sober one. The happiness of credulity is a cheap and dangerous quality.
George Bernard Shaw[32]

Organized religion is a sham and a crutch for weak-minded people who need strength in numbers.
Jesse Ventura[33]

George Bernard Shaw and Jesse Ventura echo the sentiment expressed by a lot of non-religious persons. They think we aren't any fun to be around because religion produces a kind of artificial and forced happiness. If we would let loose a little with some "real" passion, we'd all be better off. We're all focused on artificial crutches and so we don't really *get it* when it comes to passionate stuff. (We'll return in a minute to the variability Christians have shown over the years on the issue).

Are they right? *Is* Christianity a crutch? It depends on what you mean by *crutch.* My long experience suggests to me that the answer is to that question is: *Yes,* Christianity *is* a crutch, in the same way *oxygen* is a crutch, and *food* is a crutch. But not in the same way that *alcohol* is a crutch to the alcoholic. Oxygen is most definitely a crutch; but that does not make it artificial or unhealthy, as the alcoholic's dependence is artificial and unhealthy. You will not be a happy human being very long without oxygen and food, because you *need* them.

Now, you may disbelieve in Christianity and I respect that. But if you believe that the Christian kind of happiness is somehow more artificial than the "let loose" kind, I'm not sure you have thought through the issue very carefully. In fact, it is certainly debatable whether or not it succeeds in its goal – but it seems clear to me at least that the kind of happiness Christianity is trying to produce is of a deeper and more real kind.

---

of which is discussed in this chapter – that Christians are on average happier than non-Christians. While we should be careful in over-interpreting correlational evidence, this does suggest that to the degree that Christian rules differ from non-Christian rules, the Christian rules are in general encouraging rather than discouraging happiness.

Consider again the example of drinking alcohol. Is Christianity being opposed to a life of drunkenness an opposition to "real" fun and an argument in favor of a more "artificial" kind instead? No. I think if anything is true, it is the reverse of this statement. An unwillingness to drink does not keep people from having fun. People can clearly have fun without drinking. The truth is rather that the belief that *drinking is necessary for having fun* is a sure sign of someone who simply cannot have a good time otherwise.

To require alcohol in order to enjoy the company of others is to require a kind of artificial crutch.

I am not saying having fun with others while drinking is wrong; I am just saying that, if we are forced to make a comparison about which is the *real* versus *artificial* type of fun, fun that requires drinking is clearly an inferior type. To require alcohol in order to enjoy the company of others is to require a kind of artificial crutch. Real fun, then, is more likely to be had when you can enjoy the company of other people without requiring pleasure-inducing drugs.

The person who admits their idea of a good time involves getting drunk is admitting they require an artificial happiness; they are saying they cannot have fun while they are themselves; they are not only saying they cannot enjoy others while sober (an insult enough!), they are quite literally saying they cannot enjoy themselves. They must be out of their own mind to have a good time. In this and other instances, when we make this kind of judgment about the joyful, fun things in life, Christianity is consistently on the side of the "more real" kind of fun that is more likely to last.

Don't misunderstand: Christianity does not say that it is wrong to drink. But it does say it is wrong to think drinking important. Drinking should not be a necessity for joy; joy should mainly come from somewhere else. The Bible doesn't say "don't drink at all" – Jesus after all turned water into wine in John chapter 3 – but rather "do not get drunk on wine, which leads to debauchery. Instead, be filled with the Spirit, speaking to one another with psalms, hymns, and songs from the Spirit. Sing and make music from your heart to the Lord" (Ephesians 5:18-19).

Lasting Happiness Requires Other People, and Other People Require Shared Boundaries

"I wish you happiness," said the soothsayer.
Lord Shen replied: "Happiness must be taken."
From the movie *Kung Fu Panda II*[34]

We have to some degree been talking about boundaries as if they only exist for yourself. A rule about cookie dough exists so you can keep enjoying cookie dough without making yourself sick. A rule about alcohol exists to help you be able to have fun without becoming a drunkard.

And while that is true in as far as it goes, lasting happiness requires passion and fulfilled desire that is good for more than just *you*. As we discuss more in Chapter 7, no matter how much we try to believe otherwise, we need other people to be happy. If you do things that make you super-happy but make the other people around you unhappy, it is very likely your happiness will not last. Here, I want to focus only on that part of the other-people-happiness relationship that has to do with boundaries.

Think of the almost archetypal *the last biscuit on the table* problem. You are on a date at a restaurant; there is only one biscuit left; you are hungry. You recognize that there is a shared rule that suggests you should offer the biscuit to your date. But if you are like me, there is a part of you that *wants that biscuit*, and thus it would be convenient, temporarily, to ignore any thoughts about rules involving *giving*. You might say with Lord Shen in the quote above that "happiness must be taken, and my happiness is that biscuit. Move over while I eat it in front of you."

But in the long term it would be better for you to show self-denial, follow the narrow rule, and give that biscuit away. Not just *morally* better (although it would of course be that, too); I mean it would make you more happy. We will talk momentarily about the joy of giving and of the general psychological value of not thinking of yourself first; but for the moment, consider instead the more selfish joy of *having a second date*. If you are on this first date, you presumably thought this person worth dating, and would also presumably like to keep dating her. And that would undoubtedly increase in probability with your biscuit-giving behavior. And I think most people, deep down, have a sense that our happiness is interfered with by pleasure-seeking that is not bound by some kind of set of moral rules. Being happy is excellent; but *making someone happy* is even better – paradoxically, better even for you.

The Surprising Value of Not Thinking About Yourself

Given all the individualistic hype so ever-present in our culture, you might imagine that *thinking about yourself* would be a pleasant experience. And sometimes it is. But a line of research under the rubric of *objective self-awareness* suggests that self-focus is actually largely unpleasant. One study even tied it directly to self-destructive behavior: John Cheever, a mid-20th century writer famous for his self-destructive drinking, not only showed more self-focus in his writings (as measured by first-person singular pronoun use) after he became famous, but this increased self-focus was directly predictive of bouts of excessive drinking.[35] Laboratory research tells a similar story, where heightened self-focus can lead alcoholics into a drinking cycle in order to stop thinking about themselves.[36]

Now, in addition to the dangers of focusing on the self too much, it turns out that an increasing body of research reveals that *other*-focus makes people happy. Leaving that last biscuit on the table not only increases your odds of getting a second date – thereby increasing the likelihood of lasting happy relationships – it also is itself intrinsically happiness-producing. It will make you feel good because making other people happy also makes you happy. Jesus said "it is better to give than to receive," but better for whom? Better for the *giver*.

Indeed, a spate of recent research suggests the happiest people are those most likely to have personal boundaries leading to sacrifice for others.[37] It feels like a paradox. Wouldn't you be happier if you focused more on yourself? The answer: No. You are actually happier if you focus on other people. Consider that focusing on others by showing gratitude leads to more life satisfaction. For example, in one remarkable study, some participants were randomly assigned to write a letter of gratitude to someone who they felt appreciative of. This single act of expressing gratitude made participants feel happier and less depressed than a control group… and that was true even *four weeks* after they had written the letter![38]

While we should not base too much on this one study, a lot of research in multiple domains suggests that the happiest people are those who give of themselves to others. For example, one study assigned people over a 10-day period to add one of two different kinds of tasks: Some people added self-centered activities (e.g., watching TV shows they liked, getting their nails done), while others added more meaning-based activities (e.g., helping someone or cheering them up).[39] Results did not suggest that watching your favorite TV show made you unhappy – quite the contrary, there were evident psychological benefits from such self-centered behavior. Rather, the results showed that the benefits of self-centered activities tended to be more short-term, while the benefits of adding more selfless activities were more predictive of positive benefits in the long-term (in this study, the last measurement was 3 months from the end of the 10-day intervention). Other similar work suggests people who participated in a "pay it forward" intervention, involving them doing good to other people, were happier than they were before.[40]

While watching your favorite TV show will not make you unhappy, unbridled selfishness likely will. People who think *only* of themselves are on average, more likely to be unhappy. There is an irony here: They do the selfish things out of a drive for personal happiness, and yet it ultimately backfires. But it also resonates with our deepest common sense. I think most people know deep down that when they are being totally selfish they are, to borrow a quaint phrase from *Kung Fu Panda II*, trying to fill a hole that has no bottom. I think most Americans have probably experienced the deep disappointment of buying things in a selfish frenzy, only to find that the happiness it brought lasted but a day. And then they buy more things…and more…and at some point, our deeper common sense screams: "Enough! This will not satisfy." And indeed, research suggests that people who value money and possessions are less happy.[41]

Why? It is in part because those things take away from a focus on *other people*. And lasting happiness will require other people. The more we focus on our own selfish ends to the exclusion of others, the less happy we become.[xiv]

The more we focus on our own selfish ends to the exclusion of others, the less happy we become.

[xiv] I am not here directly pursuing whether Christianity is more likely to produce this outcome than atheism. As is the case with many of the principles discussed in this chapter, atheism also often emphasizes the same good behaviors and moral context. It is perhaps noteworthy, however, that as an empirical question, research on the topic does generally support the notion that religion makes people more pro-social than otherwise. Well-known researcher Scott Lilienfeld summarized this evidence: "Contrary to the forceful assertions

Aren't Christians Awfully Rule-Bound Historically?

The thoughtful reader may respond: That is all well and good but, historically, Christians seem *awfully* rule-bound, and not in a "passion-and-rules-working-together-to-create-joy" sort of way, but more like a "stodgy-people-ruining-the-fun-for-everyone" kind of way. Is it the case that a lot Christians have historically been pretty obsessed with sound prudence to the exclusion of joy?

Yes. That many facets of Christianity have over-emphasized sheer rules and de-emphasized passion – and sometimes in a mean-spirited way – is certainly true. I don't need a history lesson to know this personally. I know of modern American churches that destroy joy with an absurd focus on rules, and (drilling down further) I've known specific individuals in churches I've been a member of in the past who were like joy-killing sword-wielders. I was more than a little like that myself once, too. What are we to make of this? If Christianity emphasizes both the head and the heart, how do so many people end up as heart-killers?

Let's first consider a parallel from another kind of system: Science. One of the principles of science is an open and honest reporting of information in order to ensure both the potential for replicability and correct interpretation.[42] Does this mean scientists always engage in these practices, and there are no cultural pockets within science that have norms discouraging open reporting? Quite the contrary. Scientists are human and have many competing motivations. As a result, whole fields have developed norms that actually punish transparent reporting. There has been much discussion of this exact issue in my own specialty area of Social Psychology. Surveys have shown that alarmingly high percentages of social psychologists – sometimes almost 80% – admit to selective practices of data reporting that omit key facts or dishonestly suggest they correctly predicted something they did not actually predict.[43]

---

of some prominent atheist authors (e.g., Dawkins 2006; Dennett 2006), however, the data consistently point to a negative association between religiosity and criminal behavior and a positive association between religiosity and prosocial behavior. Both relations are modest in magnitude and ambiguous with respect to causation. At the same time, they cannot be ignored by partisans on either side of the discussion." Because a lot of that evidence was collected in Western Christian contexts, this is consistent with the general conclusion of this article that Christianity emphasizes this kind of pro-social behavior. As Lilienfeld and others have pointed out, of course, this in no way suggests that atheists are generally immoral people. My point here is to emphasize that Christianity teaches this kind of selflessness – and that selflessness is an important component of psychological health.

What are we to make of this as it relates to the connection between *Science* and the principle of open reporting? And here's my point: The fact that whole groups of people seem to fail at this principle does not mean that *Science*, as an approach to knowledge, does not *teach* the principle. Anytime you have large groups of people with competing motives, we tend to make a hash of it. The real issue is this: Does the system of belief in question support or oppose the principle in question, and thus is it possible that errors can be self-corrected from within the system itself? And are those errors, in fact, self-corrected?

And it is clear in the case of science that it can and has been self-correcting. Indeed, in my own field we have gone through several similar crises on various scientific principles and have always come out stronger.[44] And our field is currently openly debating, discussing, making changes to practices, and doing the hard work of ensuring open reporting and replication, so we can feel more confident about the results we have found.[xv]

The fact that whole groups of people seem to fail at this principle does not mean that *Science*, as an approach to knowledge, does not *teach* the principle.

The same argument applies to Christianity. Yes, there have been plenty of joy-killing churches in Christianity, perhaps even joy-killing denominations. But none of that means Christianity *teaches* joy-killing or Christ's words are not self-correcting to the Church. Words associated with the root "joy" (joy, joyful, rejoice) are used 419 times in the Bible – the vast majority of times to indicate positive endorsement of a happy state. We have already discussed Jesus' own teachings and practices on this issue directly. But it is also worth considering the following fact. Jesus generally responded well to all kinds of people: Prostitutes, tax collectors, blind people, sick people, people in the military, fishermen, random struggling women he met on his journeys…it's a long list. But there is one kind of person Jesus

---

[xv] Indeed, it is clear that much of the knowledge we produce is in fact replicable; sometimes more replicable than other scientific fields. Other fields are also going through similar crises, and science itself in the big picture has often suffered from similar issues. This discussion is not meant to cast a dispersion on social psychology research writ large, but only to point out that it is possible that norms can develop that oppose a general belief system. Because science offers plenty of reasons to change those norms, it can and is being self-corrected.

never seemed to respond particularly well to: The rule-bound joy-killers. The joy-killers of his day – a large part of the religious establishment – were the Pharisees. And among many rather scathing things he had to say about these rule experts, one is worth mentioning here (Luke 11:46): "And you experts in the law, woe to you, because you load people down with burdens they can hardly carry, and you yourselves will not lift one finger to help them."

So if you are an atheist or skeptic reading this, and you wonder why you meet some joyless Christian rule-followers on your journey, I would say to you that this is not what Christianity is *trying* to produce. And if you are one of those joyless Christian rule-followers yourself (as I once was), I would suggest the useful expedient of heeding our Lord's own words: Attend to more than just rules, and learn to find the joy He speaks of.

So it is important to acknowledge the contribution of joy-killing Christians to the general perception that we are over-rule bound. However, part of this belief likely exists for a different reason: Because sometimes the Bible makes different statements to meet different people where they are – and some of those statements can seem to exclude joy entirely when taken alone. Think of parenting two different children, one of whom can't seem to follow any rules, and the other of whom is so obsessed with rules they drain the life out of everything and everyone. The parents may have the same *goal* for both children – the happy integration of perfect morality and perfect passion – but it is unlikely that their conversations with each child would be at all similar. Would it make sense for the parents to spend hours talking to their rule-bound child about the importance of following rules? Doubtful. They'd probably talk to that child about the importance of joy. Would it make sense for the parents to send their rule-breaking child to a seminar titled *How to Experience Freedom from Rules*? Maybe not the most useful idea. Better to spend time explaining how they could probably use a bit more structure in their lives and the value of upholding rules.

The same principle applies here. Just as there have been churches that excluded joy, there have also been churches that worshipped pleasure to the exclusion of moral rules. One of them is directly discussed in the Bible itself. The Corinthian church was a rule-less mess, and thus when Paul wrote to them, he naturally was more inclined to chastise them for a lack of attention to rules, as in this passage from 1 Corinthians 5:1-2: "It is actually reported that there is sexual immorality among you, and of a kind that even pagans do not tolerate: A man is sleeping with his father's wife. And you are proud! Shouldn't you rather have gone into mourning and have put out of your fellowship the man who has been doing this?" If all that you read was this kind of admonition of Paul to the Corinthian church – and there are many such admonitions – you might falsely believe Paul was simply about exacting rules on the church.

But you'd be wrong about that. Consider that the Galatian church had a different problem – they were obsessed with rules. Paul wrote fully three chapters to them (Galatians chapters 3, 4, and 5) to try to get them out of that obsession, imploring them to not take rules about circumcision and seasonal festivals (and so forth) quite so seriously. In fact, in Galatians 5:1, he goes so far as comparing their obsession for these rules to slavery: "It is for freedom that Christ has set us free. Stand firm, then, and do not let yourselves be burdened again by a yoke of slavery." Again, if all you read was those three chapters, you might get the impression Paul was really, really anti-rule. But he isn't; he's just meeting the problems the Galatians are actually having where they are.

And in fact, Paul discusses his desire for the Corinthians' joy (2 Corinthians 1:24) and for the Galatians to not use their freedom to break God's laws (Galatians 5:13-15). In just the way a frustrated parent might qualify statements to a rule-breaking child ("we want you to have joy, child, but your rule-breaking has got to stop because you are hurting people") or to a rule-obsessed child ("we want you to keep doing good, child, but you are becoming so obsessed with the rules that you can't experience joy"), Paul reveals both sides of this issue to everyone: He just directs his remarks to the specific needs at each church.

It is also worth noting that, in the big picture, part of the response to the argument about individual churches or people being joy-killers is empirical. On balance, a lot of evidence in general (and about Christianity in particular) suggests that religious people are in fact happier, better adjusted, and more pro-social.[45] This evidence was compelling enough to inspire a new "Atheism 3.0" movement that argues the benefits of religiosity are so powerful that people should believe in God even though God doesn't really exist.[46] Thus, while it is clearly the case that there is quite a bit of variability across both religious and irreligious people, there is certainly enough evidence that Christians are joy-inspirers to validate the basic conclusions of this chapter.

The Conclusion: A Picture of Lasting Happiness

In one of my own long-enduring traditions, I have watched the classic movie *How the Grinch Stole Christmas* every holiday season for each of the past 33 years. In that movie, the grumpy Grinch steals every last thing he can from the *Whos* on Christmas Eve. He takes their presents, trees, decorations, food – everything.

You see, the Grinch was absolutely, positively certain that stealing all the *stuff* surrounding their favorite holiday would make them miserable. Oh, how he wanted them to be miserable! And every single year of my life since I was 12, I have cried at what happened when the Grinch goes to enjoy his triumph by listening to the misery of the Whos without their presents[47]:

And he did hear a sound rising over the snow.
It started in low, then it started to grow.
But this sound wasn't sad!
Why, this sound sounded glad!
Every Who down in Whoville, the tall and the small,
Was singing. Without any presents at all!
He hadn't stopped Christmas from coming! It came!
Somehow or other, it came just the same!

You see, the Whos in Whoville had a happiness that *lasts.* It was not dependent on circumstances or presents or beer or anything else. It wasn't some fragile thing that faded with the end of a binge-watching TV show escapade, or required every single detail of every experience to be *just so.*

And *that* is the picture I see in the Bible; the picture that Christianity is trying to produce. In a passage that in many ways is strangely similar to *Whoville*, in Acts 16:22-25, the Grinches of Paul and Silas' world tried to take away their joy and happiness by removing all their stuff and surroundings:

Then the multitude rose up together against them; and the magistrates tore off their clothes and commanded them to be beaten with rods. And when they had laid many stripes on them, they threw them into prison, commanding the jailer to keep them securely. Having received such a charge, he put them into the inner prison and fastened their feet in the stocks.

You'd think they'd be pretty down after that. But watch what happens next (emphasis mine):

But at midnight Paul and Silas were ***singing hymns to God****, and the prisoners were listening to them.*

Paul and Silas had everything taken from them, and yet they were – like the Whos – *singing. They* had found some kind of happiness that lasts.

And *that* is precisely what this chapter is about. It is about what produces a happiness that lasts. And while the answer to that question is complicated, and we've only hit on one part of it, it is nonetheless true that my own experience teaches me that Christian principles of happiness match the landscape of lasting happiness.

Calling Us Back To the Bigger Picture

Faith: The effort to believe that which your common sense tells you is not true.
Elbert Hubbard, in *The Atheist's Bible*[48]

Atheists such as Elbert Hubbard often chastise Christians for our abandonment of common sense. But actually, Christianity rather vigorously defends common sense. Indeed, as part of this chapter illustrates, what Jesus largely tries to do is get you to follow and live up to your own common-sense moral compass with respect to boundaries.

There is a sense that we are motivated to ignore the main messages of this chapter. After all, sacrificing and self-control are almost by definition at least partially unpleasant. I feel it, too. Many days I'd prefer to watch Star Wars movies and eat Snickers bars until my pants bust, and not care about anyone or anything else.

Yet I think most people are intuitively aware of the value of boundaries; we just often would prefer, in the short term, to ignore them. Boundaries may be good; boundaries may produce a long-term well of happiness; but there is no denying that boundaries are darned inconvenient. And it is our insistence on ignoring the Christian teachings imploring *self-control* that ultimately leads us against our own better wisdom. Our short-term desires often overwhelm even our own long-term selfish interests, but most people, somewhere, deep down, have a sense that we cannot be satisfied by mere selfish behavior – and Christianity, in telling us it is better to give than receive, it is better to die to our temptations than to give in to them, is simply calling us back to what we already know. It is calling us out of our momentary desires to look at our life in the large picture. It is trying to replace the Grinch's vision with the Whos' vision.

Christianity helps the human machine run well by providing a complex roadmap to help us navigate the tensions between boundaries and passion. In doing so, it aims to make the experience of life simpler. As an example, consider the case of an alcoholic I know named "Bob." Bob's simple devotion to temporal fun at all costs ultimately made him less free to enjoy almost anything else. And as a result, Bob's simple pursuit of alcoholic pleasure made his life very complicated. In fact, Bob had to constantly lie, cheat, compromise, apologize, and numerous other difficult things in order to even have a relationship with his spouse, and his boundary-free devotion to drinking eventually led to other horrible and complex things like divorce and alimony. For Bob, the result of a simple approach to pleasure was not only that he didn't feel a whole lot of pleasure, but also that his life actually became more complicated. Whereas if Bob had followed the more complex approach to boundaries suggested in this chapter, he would have likely had many more hours of his life where he went home, opened the door, and greeted his happy wife in a simple fashion.[xvi]

So when atheists argue that Christianity is harmful to humanity because it is oppressive and restrictive, I'm not sure they've totally thought out what they are saying. If our rules produced no good lasting results on human health and psychology, why are Christians so happy on average? Our rules maintain both freedom and boundaries. These rules are not designed to remove freedom – they are designed to stop people from abusing freedom by hurting themselves and others, and in that sense to keep freedom and happiness for the long haul.

[xvi] This is not to imply that non-alcoholics all have happy marriages, or that relationships are not complex in other ways. It is only to point out a principle which Christianity teaches and in which I have found to be true: A complex approach to boundaries and passion leads to behavioral simplicity. In the example raised here, I am certain that, isolated from all other variables, the Christian approach to navigating boundaries and passion would have produced – for that issue – more long-term simple happiness than otherwise.

Christian rules are not designed to stop people from eating cookie dough – they are designed to stop people from getting so sick from cookie dough that they can't enjoy it, and to be sure there is enough cookie dough to go around for more than just yourself. And a lot of evidence suggests that Christians really *do* enjoy pleasures more than other people – because our pleasures don't eventually make us sick. Because we believe we are listening to the God who made both the pleasures and us, we hardly find this fact surprising.

CHAPTER FIVE
PRAYER MEETS THE PLOW: THE PSYCHOLOGY OF MEANING

With God nothing is empty of meaning, nothing without symbolism.
St. Irenaeus[1]

I will imagine that my soul and body are like the two hands of a compass.
St. Anthony Mary Claret[2]

The almighty and most holy Word of the Father pervades the whole of reality, everywhere unfolding his power and shining on all things visible and invisible.
St. Athanasius[3]

In the classic Christmas movie *Miracle on 34th Street*, the Supreme Court of New York is forced to decide whether a man who claims to be Santa Claus is, in fact, the *real* Santa Claus. I have watched quite a few courtroom dramas in my day, and I can honestly say that it is almost never the case that the primary question floating around the witness box is whether Santa Claus is a real person sitting in the courtroom. And yet there it was: A handful of attorneys arguing about it just as if they were trying to decide on the validity of Miranda Rights.

Susan Walker, a child in the movie whose mother had raised her to disbelieve in such things, struggles with whether or not Santa Claus is a real person—even as evidence pointing that direction curiously begins to mount. At one point, she asks the man who claims to be Santa Claus to give her a real house. When he hedges, she says matter-of-factly: "If you're really Santa Claus, you can get it for me. And if you can't, you're only a nice man with a white beard like mother says."

Even reading those words right now years later, I can feel the mingling of common sense, yearning, and heartbreak in her voice. Susan *wants* to believe in Santa Claus—but it seems so unlikely—but oh, imagine if he really *were* Santa Claus! Isn't it truly disappointing to think he is just one more nice man with a white beard? Wouldn't it be wonderful if… if… but surely that's all he is. There can't *really* be a Santa Claus… can there?

I think a lot of people who *dis*believe in Santa Claus are pulling for him anyway. They hold a secret dream that maybe, against all odds, Kris Kringle really *will* prove himself and give the girl her house. I think that's why movies like that are so popular—after all, that's exactly what happens at the end of the movie. The skeptic realizes there is some truth to fairytales, there really is more to this life than what we see, and Susan gets her house.

I don't believe in Santa Claus. I believe in something better. I believe in a world where everything is more than meets the eye, where anything is possible, and where there is a happy ending. That is the vision cast by Christianity—a vision of a world where atoms and fairies meet, where prayers and plows work together, where everything has *meaning*. In this chapter, we're going to explore both the prayer-meets-plow Christian vision and contrast it to the alternative vision currently being cast by atheists.

Of Atoms and Fairytales

To say people desire meaningfulness in life is to state something unarguably true.[4] To say people enjoy discovering the 'meaning of life' is practically an axiom. Very few people I know would choose the hollow empty void of a solely material universe over the mystical beauty of a fairytale. (Some people say they would—and we will return later in this chapter to the vision cast by atheists and compare it to the Christian vision.)

That is probably why a large portion of the world's population is religious—they find their *meaning* in it. Atheist Daniel Dennett sums this up:

> *According to surveys, most of the people of the world say religion is very important in their lives. Many of these people would say that without their religion their lives would be meaningless.*[5]

I think that's right. And I think whether religious or irreligious, there is a tendency in us to *want* magic and mystery; we'd love to believe in Santa Claus. Even in mostly-secular Great Britain, the populace voted—twice, and both times over the objections of the so-called intellectual elite—that the fairy world of Tolkien's *The Lord of the Rings* was their favorite British novel ever.[6] Even secular atheists seem to long for things to be more than they seem.

The Fairyland of Christianity

He has also set eternity in the human heart; yet no one can fathom what God has done from beginning to end.
Ecclesiastes 3:11

I will give you hidden treasures, riches stored in secret places, so that you may know that I am the Lord, the God of Israel, who summons you by name.
Isaiah 45:3

[T]he fullness of him who fills everything in every way.
Ephesians 1:22-23

For every house is built by someone, but God is the builder of everything.
Hebrews 3:4

For in him all things were created: things in heaven and on earth, visible and invisible, whether thrones or powers or rulers or authorities; all things have been created through him and for him. He is before all things, and in him all things hold together.
Colossians 1:16 17

Jesus looked at them and said, "With man this is impossible, but not with God; all things are possible with God."
Mark 10:27

He reveals deep and hidden things; he knows what lies in darkness, and light dwells with him.
Daniel 2:22

I will also give that person a white stone with a new name written on it, known only to the one who receives it.
Revelation 2:17

This desire for another world is exactly what Christianity expects; in Christian thought, God *put* the desire there. Ponder for a minute the litany of verses above. The Christian Scriptures are practically bursting with secret names, hidden knowledge, with impossibilities made possible, with mountains moved and diseases cured and ancient dreams fulfilled. It is a world where all things, invisible and visible—stuff of atoms and the stuff of fairyland—are created and held together by God. It is a world where His unseen spirit permeates every leaf, every ocean sunset, every baby's cry, every sad note of a violin.

Given this, it is unsurprising to find a sense in the Bible that we are to approach this world with childlike wonder. You can practically feel Jesus' giddiness in this fact in Luke 10:21:

> *At that time Jesus, full of joy through the Holy Spirit, said, "I praise you, Father, Lord of heaven and earth, because you have hidden these things from the wise and learned, and revealed them to little children. Yes, Father, for this is what you were pleased to do."*

Jesus was full of joy at the fact that little children knew stuff that adults could not know. It isn't made clear what that knowledge is—but nonetheless, it is clear that the world of Jesus is a miraculous place that requires some trust that *something* exists that we cannot see. Ours is a world bursting with meaning around every corner, because our reality and our existence have an Author.

The Christian Scriptures are practically bursting with secret names, hidden knowledge, with impossibilities made possible, with mountains moved and diseases cured and ancient dreams fulfilled.

The Plow of Christianity

Take from the church the miraculous, the supernatural, the incomprehensible, the unreasonable, the impossible, the unknowable, the absurd, and nothing but a vacuum remains.

Robert G. Ingersoll, from *The Atheist's Bible*[7]

Now few people would deny that Christianity teaches a belief in the miraculous, that we argue for a belief in things beyond this world, or that we relish in the invisible. But a lot of people—such as atheist Robert Ingersoll—think that is *all* it teaches. They think Christianity offers nothing beyond a fairy world they do not themselves believe in.

I don't think most atheists actually believe Christianity doesn't teach about atoms and earth—we'll deal with what I think they do mean in a second. But for the record, Christianity has always encouraged a belief in both the reality of another world *and* the reality of *this* world. Yes, Jesus said in Luke 12:23 that "Life is more than food; the body is more than clothes." But Jesus didn't say "life is more than food, so you don't need to eat." No, He told us God knew we needed food, too: In the same passage (Luke 12:30), Jesus said "your Father knows that you need" food and clothes. Life is more than food, but it isn't less. This is the history of Christian teaching in a nutshell. Christianity has long denied that this physical world is all there is, but it also refutes those who argue that life is *all* spirit and the stuff of earth is therefore meaningless.

I think most atheists would likely grant that this is what Christianity teaches in the abstract. What I think they mean in their attack is something more like this: You Christians have your heads in the clouds so much that you don't actually *do* anything useful. Your 'fairyland' substitutes fiction for truth and keeps you from focusing on the positive value of making the physical world a better place.

Consider these quotes from atheist authors and web sites:

The inventor of the plow did more good than the maker of the first rosary—because, say what you will, plowing is better than praying.
Robert G. Ingersoll, from *The Atheist's Bible*[8]

Lighthouses are more helpful than churches.
Ben Franklin, from *The Atheist's Bible*[9]

Two hands working can do more than a thousand clasped in prayer.
Unknown[10]

The sailor does not pray for wind, he learns to sail.
Gustaf Lindborg[11]

An Atheist believes that a hospital should be built instead of a church. An Atheist believes that deed must be done instead of a prayer said. An Atheist

strives for involvement in life and not escape into death. He wants disease conquered, poverty vanished, war eliminated.
Justin Brown[12]

If you're an atheist, you know, you believe, this is the only life you're going to get. It's a precious life. It's a beautiful life. It's something we should live to the full, to the end of our days. Where if you're religious and you believe in another life somehow, that means you don't live this life to the full because you think you're going to get another one. That's an awfully negative way to live a life. Being an atheist frees you up to live this life properly, happily and fully.
Richard Dawkins[13]

The tenor of those quotes is not so much that Christians don't believe in the value of lighthouses, but rather that lighthouse building is somehow in conflict with the needs of the church. That if we had less religion, we'd have more hospitals, less disease, less war, better farming—because religion distracts us from those things. In the vernacular of the old expression, we are too heavenly-minded to do any earthly good. We don't live meaningful lives on earth because we think something beyond the earth exists.

Because atheists focus intently on science and have started to convince popular culture that Christianity stops scientific progress due to our focus on fairyland, I think it's worth pausing for a minute to throw some facts into the equation. Consider that famous atheist Richard Dawkins once said:

> "People like to say that faith and science can live together side by side, but I don't think they can. They're deeply opposed. Science is a discipline of investigation and constructive doubt, questioning with logic, evidence and reason to draw conclusions. Faith, by stark contrast, demands a positive suspension of critical faculties."[14]

You, too, may have an impression that Christianity is opposed to science. I have spent a bit of time already trying to counter that impression in Chapter Three. But here let's briefly consider a history of prayer versus the plow—does Christianity cause people to abandon practical and useful earthly studies?

I'm tempted to focus only on myself. (Don't laugh—I don't mean *in general*, I mean in this specific instance). I am a scientist; I have made impassioned arguments on my blog in favor of empiricism, and so the attack on my religion on grounds of incompatibility with science naturally strikes me as hollow. I'm tempted to spend quite a bit of time explaining how, not only does it not occur to me to think science and religion are incompatible, but how my faith has made me a better scientist in a variety of ways. I grant that specific religious groups sometimes oppose specific scientific findings and vice versa, but that fact alone is hardly meaningful in the grander scheme. Certain scientific groups oppose other scientific groups, yet no one is clamoring to ditch science as a result. The whole attack is as odd to me as the idea of a chair attacking its own legs.

However, I do realize my perspective isn't the only one out there—so I think it's useful to pause for a moment to consider the history of science and philosophy through a slightly larger lens.

Famous Christian Intellectuals

To accomplish this, below I present a list of scientists, mathematicians, and philosophers who identified as Christian. In each case, I also present a brief summary of their achievements.

Let me tell you what I'm *not* trying to accomplish with this list. I'm most definitely not saying that atheists don't contribute to science. They do. In fact, they contribute to it in ways disproportionate to the relative size of their population (a disproportionate number of atheists have won Nobel Prizes, for example). Atheists have historically been intelligent people, and I respect that.

My goal, rather, is this: Atheists sometimes claim Christians are stupidly non-empirical, and our culture has started to absorb this negative tendency. They think we are *just* living in fairyland. I don't entirely blame the atheists—there are certainly plenty of stupidly non-empirical Christians out there. The Church must own up to that. But my point is simply this: That fact is more because *people in general* (of any ilk, religious or irreligious) can sometimes be stupidly impractical than it is because Christianity systematically produces them. Christianity isn't, as a *thing,* incompatible with science, as a *thing.* If you believe that, it is an honest question to ask yourself as a thinking person: Why, if Christianity is so incompatible with science, have Christians founded so many scientific disciplines? Why have we contributed so much to scientific knowledge—if our focus on prayer really does prohibit the plow?

Inclusion Criteria

People often want to "claim" famous people on *their side,* and thus there is sometimes debate about whether someone was or wasn't a believer of X. That has also been the case with many presumed Christians or atheists. I have heard Christians claim that Darwin was a believing religious person late in his life (seems clearly ludicrous based on what I've read) or atheists claim that C.S. Lewis was anti-religious late in his life (equally ludicrous based on my research).

What I'm saying is that I don't trust other people very much. So, for this list below, I didn't rely on some other person's list—I investigated each of these people to determine whether or not they were Christian. My criteria were that they had to personally profess to the Christian faith, be at least partially active in a Christian church, and hold to more or less orthodox Christian beliefs in line with commonly-accepted Christian creeds. So, for example, Isaac Newton was a devoutly religious man who wrote more about theology than science, but he held to some views that are widely accepted to be at odds with the basic Christian faith. Therefore, he didn't make the list.

Now, history is a hard thing to read. There is no doubt in my mind that if you raised all of the people on this list from the dead and asked them what they really believed, a few of them would say "no, you idiot, I didn't believe Christianity." At the edges of the list, there is certainly room for disagreement. I don't provide this as a definitive list for all time; I'm not a historian. I am aware that in some cultures it would have been disastrous for people to admit they weren't religious and sometimes that affects the read of history.

That said, I would be shocked if we raised all these people from the dead to find that the majority of them were non-believers. I would expect that, in the main, this list represents a group of people who were mostly religious, mostly Christian—and yet still excellent intellectuals who are widely recognized as such by everyone, including secular culture. Regardless, it is still worth asking the question *why did science grow so intensely within Christian culture, if Christianity is so opposed to science?*

As additional external validation of the greatness of the thinkers on this list, occasionally below I will reference a few "top thinkers/influential people of all time" lists. Those come from the following sources, all of which include secular and religious persons:

Why did science grow so intensely within Christian culture, if Christianity is so opposed to science?

The Greatest Minds and Ideas of All Time by Will Durant.[15]

The 100: A Ranking of the Most Influential Persons in History by Michael H. Hart.[16]

Top 50 Geniuses of All Time by 4 Mind 4 Life Blog.[17]

As you'll see below, I also make references to other markers of greatness, such as their appearance on a postage stamp (in mostly secular societies, I should add)—I figure if your country puts you on a postage stamp, you must be famous!—and having Star Trek ships and cities named after them.

Scientists, Mathematicians, and Philosophers Who Were (or Are) Christians

- *Michael Faraday*: Electromagnetic theorist; credited with the "Faraday effect" relating to the interaction of light and magnetic force; Top 100 most influential; Top 50 thinkers; on a postage stamp.
- *James Clerk Maxwell*: Poll showed him to be 3rd most influential physicist of all time, behind Einstein and Newton; Top 100 most influential; on a postage stamp; Einstein said of his work that it was the "most profound and the most fruitful that physics has experienced since the time of Newton." Einstein reportedly had pictures of both Maxwell and Faraday on his desk.
- *William Thomas Kelvin*: Invented the Kelvin system of temperature measurement.
- *Gregor Mendel*: Founder of modern genetics; Top 100 most influential; on a postage stamp.
- *George Stokes*: Credited with "Stokes Law" relating to frictional force.

- *Max Planck*: Founder of quantum theory; Nobel Prize winner in 1918; Top 100 most influential; on a postage stamp.
- *Robert Boyle*: Founder of modern Chemistry; credited with "Boyle's law" relating to gas pressure; Top 50 thinkers; on a postage stamp.
- *Blaise Pascal*: Contributor to much of modern mathematics; Top 50 thinkers; on a postage stamp.
- *Gottfried Wilhelm Leibniz*: Credited in part with inventing calculus; Top 50 thinkers; on a postage stamp.
- *Francis Bacon*: Founder of the scientific method; Top 100 most influential; on a postage stamp.
- *Francis Collins:* Head of Genome Project; won "Presidential Medal of Freedom" for his scientific work—highest U.S. civilian honor; current NIH director.
- *Werner Heisenberg:* 1932 Nobel Prize for physics; founder of quantum mechanics; credited with the "Heisenberg uncertainty principle;" Top 100 most influential; on a postage stamp; said, "the first gulp from the glass of natural sciences will turn you into an atheist, but at the bottom of the glass God is waiting for you."
- *James Prescott Joule:* "Joule's Law" of energy, thermodynamics.
- *Louis Pasteur*: One of the founders of Microbiology; Top 100 most influential people; on a postage stamp; had a ship named after him in Star Trek.
- *Johannes Kepler*: One of the most famous astronomers ever; credited with "Kepler's laws of planetary motion;" on a postage stamp.
- *The Wright Brothers*: Inventor of airplane; Top 100 most influential; on a postage stamp.
- *Antoine-Laurent de Lavoisier*: Father of modern chemistry; Top 100 most influential; on a postage stamp.
- *John Dalton*: Contributed to atomic theory and colorblindness research; has a unit of atomic measurement named after him AND the French word for color-blindness; Top 100 most influential.
- *Antonie Philips van Leeuwenhoek*: Credited as the "Father of Microbiology;" Top 100 most influential; on a postage stamp.

- *Guglielmo Marconi*: Inventor of the radio; Top 100 most influential; on a postage stamp.
- *Alexander Fleming*: Discovered penicillin; Top 100 most influential; on a postage stamp.
- *Joseph Lister*: Founder of antiseptic surgery; Top 100 most influential; on a postage stamp.
- *Edward Jenner*: Discovered smallpox vaccine; Top 100 most influential; on a postage stamp.
- *Leonhard Euler*: Mathematics; introduced a lot of mathematical terminology; credited with "Euler's number;" on a postage stamp.
- *Thomas Malthus*: Sociologist and economist who influenced Darwin; founder of Demography; Top 100 most influential.
- *George Washington Carver*: Promoter of alternative crop practices and inventor of peanut butter; on a postage stamp.
- *David Livingstone*: Geographer of Africa; fellow of prestigious Royal Geographical Society of London; on a postage stamp.
- *Samuel Morse*: Inventor of the telegraph; on a postage stamp.
- *William of Ockham*: Philosopher credited with the principle of parsimony, or "Ockham's razor;" credited with the concept of separation of Church and State.
- *Søren Kierkegaard*: Founded existential philosophy; on a postage stamp.
- *George Berkeley*: Famous philosopher of subjective experience; Top 50 thinkers; on a postage stamp; City of Berkeley, California named after him.
- *St. Thomas Aquinas*: Famous philosopher; Top 50 thinkers; on a postage stamp.
- *René Descartes*: Famous philosopher who founded Analytic Geometry; top 100 most influential; Top 50 thinkers; on a postage stamp.

That list is a *who's who* of the scientific and philosophical world. It includes a large number of intellectuals who founded whole fields of science or philosophy, who made important scientific discoveries, or who invented really important practical things. I will forgo focusing on the parable we might draw from the fact (to be discussed in my upcoming book *Tales from the Ironic*) that anti-religious Berkeley, California is named after devout Christian George Berkeley, and instead ask you to consider this. Atheists sometimes claim we in the church are no good to the world because we ignore earth and plow, the hospital and atom, in favor of prayer and fairytales and spirit. In fact, a large part of their case against us rests simply on the idea that our religion causes us to live bereft of a sense of the here and now. And if you think that's true, then you should imagine your life without penicillin or airplanes or antiseptics or smallpox vaccines. All of those things were invented by Christians who were working with atoms—the stuff of earth in the physical world.

Perhaps atheists would have eventually made the above discoveries if Christians had not, but that isn't my point. My point is that the atheist accusation implies that the Church is *antithetical* to intellectual pursuits—and this accusation must face the stark reality that Christians founded a huge percentage of the natural sciences, mathematics, existential philosophy, and a great deal more. Indeed, Christians continue to make ground-breaking discoveries today. The accusation that we have ignored the lighthouse and hospital and plow in favor of prayer is purely fiction. We haven't.

Integrating Atoms and Fairyland: The Christian Vision

Food in dreams appears like our food awake; yet the sleepers are not nourished by it, for they are asleep.
St. Augustine, *Confessions*[18]

The heavens declare the glory of God;
the skies proclaim the work of his hands.
Day after day they pour forth speech;
night after night they reveal knowledge.
They have no speech, they use no words;
no sound is heard from them.
Yet their voice goes out into all the earth,
their words to the ends of the world. Psalm 19:1-4

I sometimes imagine my life as a fairytale. In this fairytale vision, my world is peopled with a litany of amazing things. I am king of a castle; a beautiful queen sits at my side. A tiny fairy-elf daughter plays and laughs and dances at my feet. Mountains climb thousands of miles into endless skies. Plains stretch out forever like a lonely heartache. Trees seem to call to some long-lost lover. Even the rocks seem to be crying for something.

Fairytales almost always involve tragedy; and my own fairytale wasn't always so full of castles and beautiful queens and fairy-elves as it is now. It had its share of tragedy, too. In fact, for a long time my life was a long sad tale of a ne'er-do-well who had betrayed his own king. I was a perfectly normal boy who had volunteered for the post of Sauron or Tash or the wicked witch a hundred times over. I tried – unsuccessfully – to kill my king. And my actions led to what often seems to happen to the "bad guys": I was caught, beaten up, betrayed in turn by the very things I had abandoned goodness to treasure, and left for dead; a lonesome, angry, pathetic, helpless man, sitting alone in a prison cell of his own creation, mired in muck and filth and starving for real food, waiting like Haman to face the gallows I had built. The gallows I deserved.

And then something amazing happened. The king who I had betrayed stormed into my cell on a white horse. I could still see the wounds from where I had stabbed him. I expected the worst. I deserved the worst. Then I saw in his eyes what I did not and still do not comprehend: mercy… hope… forgiveness... kindness… love. He should have tortured and killed me. Instead he pulled me out of my cell, gave me a room in his palace, fed me the best of food and drink, offered me the best of everything there is under the sun. I succumbed to this love without understanding it. I had been freed. And I am living happily ever after.

Now of course there is a sense in which this fairytale vision is simply a fantasy overlaid on top of the more mundane-sounding facts with which I normally describe my world. I do not think that believing in *that* story literally is a path to sanity. And you will be happy to know I have yet to introduce my wife at church by saying "Here is Queen Kathrene, bow to her, knaves." I rarely, if ever, say to my colleagues at the end of a faculty meeting, "Lo, I go to my castle to spend time with a small fairy-elf. We shall play the ancient game known in my kingdom as…Mario Kart."[xvii]

[xvii] To be fair, and in acknowledgment of my wonderful and patient colleagues, I *have* said some pretty wacky things at faculty meetings.

And yet, there is a sense in which this vision, though not literally true, is nonetheless a true representation of some deeper *feeling* about my life that is hard to express otherwise. The facts of my life are just facts, but my fairytale vision expresses the *meaning* of those facts. I have a wife, yes: But she feels like a radiant queen. I have a daughter, true enough: But she *feels* like a fairy-princess. I have a house: But it *feels* like a glorious realm.

Facts are not the intended end of any good story. They are *carriers*; they are *mediators*; they are *pointers*. I sometimes feel that part of our temptation on this earth is to, quite literally, miss the point. It is to miss the thing that all these facts are pointing at, to deny the wonder and mystery and deep-rooted feelings we all have that there is something more to our universe than what we see. That is the fairytale. We are all living in it. The Psalmist in the opening quote did *not* say *that sky is an illusion*—rather he said that very real sky *speaks to us* of something else, of a glory from God that is unseen. The sky is real enough; the problem is that we might stop there if we don't hear its voice pointing to something else, too.

Facts are not the intended end of any good story.

A Fairytale Come True

But this is only getting over the difficulty of describing peacock green by calling it blue… No man could say how far his animal dread of the end was mixed up with mystical traditions touching morals and religion. It is exactly because these things are animal, but not quite animal, that the dance of all the difficulties begins. The materialists analyze the easy part, deny the hard part, and go home to their tea.

G. K. Chesterton[19]

Christianity quite literally claims to be a fairy-tale-come true—a fairytale that occupies the world of atoms. Christianity is the literal integration of earth and heaven. Thousands of years before Christ came, the world's literature had cried out of death and resurrection. As C.S. Lewis pointed out in his book *Miracles*,[20] ancient mythology spoke of corn-kings and wine-gods who died and then rose again. The world's literature aches with stories of simple conditions set and then broken by choice, and Pandora's box of evil unleashed. The world's literature bubbles with stories of secret doors and worlds behind worlds and all sorts of other wondrous things. And Christianity says: All those desires, all those hopes do not exist without meaning; they will be fulfilled. Pandora's box *was* opened by human choice, but the Corn-King has come to overcome its death and offer new life. And there is a secret world of goodness and hope and mercy and love; the Corn-King opened the door into it. You may taste its wonder, feel its warmth, be awed by its beauty.

Christianity is thus a story. And because we believe in a story—and not just a set of facts—we assume that the parts of the story have meaning above and beyond themselves. The materialist says that water exists as water for only one purpose—to satisfy physical thirst. But Christianity says that, yes, it exists for that purpose, but not *only* for that purpose. It also exists to represent something else, something different, something of which the water itself is but a foretaste. Baptism is a physical event, with physical water. But, for the Christian, it represents something else, something real, something eternal about the cleansing and renewal of the human soul. That is more complex. We acknowledge the reality of physical reality, but also a *different* reality as well. Atoms and fairies meet.[xviii]

The Fairytale of the Creed

Consider the Christian Creed. Christian churches have explicitly endorsed this Creed in some form for 1700 years. It defines what Christians have always believed since Jesus was on the earth. Here it is in its most basic form (a version commonly known as the Apostle's Creed[21]):

[xviii] Throughout this chapter, I paint a dichotomy between materialist atheists who do not believe in fairyland and Christians who do believe in it. This is just a picture – one that has been used before in other apologetic works such as G.K. Chesterton's *Orthodoxy* – but I am of course aware that Christianity does not literally teach that fairies exist (and I personally think the traditional "fairies" of those stories are not likely representative of real beings). Also, it is possible for materialist atheists to believe in something *like* a fairy as long as it exists as a physical being. These qualifications are important, but the larger point of this metaphor nonetheless remains – the spirit of the fairytale is to ascribe deeper meaning to physical events. Christianity provides a framework consistent with this idea, while materialistic atheism does not.

I believe in God, the Father Almighty, maker of heaven and earth. And in Jesus Christ, his only Son, our Lord, who was conceived by the Holy Spirit, and born of the virgin Mary, suffered under Pontius Pilate, was crucified, died and was buried. He descended into hell. On the third day He rose again from the dead. He ascended into heaven and sits at the right hand of God the Father Almighty. From thence He will come to judge the living and the dead. I believe in the Holy Spirit, the holy Christian church, the communion of saints, the forgiveness of sins, the resurrection of the body, and the life everlasting.

The Creed is not a list of rules. It is light on abstract truths. Rather, it is a *story*—a story of a perfect God who, out of love for us, His creation, took on human form in order to die on our behalf. It is like a fairytale, like Eugene giving his life for the lost princess in *Tangled* or the Beast giving his life for Belle in *Beauty and the Beast.* A loving King gives up everything to save his lost bride. *This is Christianity.*[xix]

The Creed is not a list of rules. It is light on abstract truths. Rather, it is a *story*—a story of a perfect God who, out of love for us, His creation, took on human form in order to die on our behalf.

Only, Christianity isn't just a beautiful love story; it's a *true* love story. Jesus isn't just some god of ancient mythology. He is a real person documented in Jewish history. He lived and did real things. That's the Christian Creed. *That's* what you must believe to be a Christian.

That's not *all* Christians believe, of course. But most of the other beliefs are things most everyone believes anyway. Christians believe murder is wrong. So does almost everyone. Christians believe cheating on your spouse is wrong. So do most people. Christians believe you should give to those less fortunate than yourselves. But pretty much every belief system in the world worth its salt teaches the same thing.

[xix] The Apostle's Creed is a shorter (and more pervasively used) version of the Nicene Creed. The Nicene Creed (so named because of its origins at the Council of Nicaea in 325 AD) is very similar in content to, but partially expands upon, the Apostle's Creed. A full discussion of these Creeds is beyond the scope of this book, but the interested reader can see a series of pieces I have written on the Christian Creeds at apologeticprofessor.com/articles. For our purposes, any of the basic instantiations of the Creed would lead to the same conclusions drawn in this chapter.

Why is that? I mean, why do Christians focus less on abstract principles and rules and laws and more on what can only be described as a story? Because God isn't a set of abstract principles. He's a… *Person.* God isn't a *what* but a *Who.* The Author of our story gave us *personal meaning.* God didn't create you to be a concept of abstract mathematics or theology. He made you for *relationship.* He wants to *know you* and for you to *know Him.* You can't be known via a mathematical equation, because you aren't a number. That is why the Bible doesn't read like a textbook, why Jesus didn't teach in mathematical formulas but in stories. Descriptions of relationships between two people do not read like biology textbooks… they read like fairytales.

A World Without Fairyland: Comparing Atheists' Alternative Vision to the Christian Vision

Isn't it enough to see that a garden is beautiful without having to believe that there are fairies at the bottom of it too?
Douglas Adams, from *The Atheist's Bible*[22]

I am tempted to respond to atheist Douglas Adams' reasonable question like this: *No, Douglas, it is not enough. I tried that. Take something I love even more than gardens: mountains. Well, I tried being as close to them as I could, hiking on them, camping on them, feeling their dirt in my hands, seeing their majesty in as many ways as I could. I gave it all I had to appreciate their beauty. And in the end, it simply wasn't enough. I wanted something more than they could give. The beauty of mountains and gardens is either a passing fancy that doesn't ultimately provide contentment, or it is pointing to something that does. But I'm certain it isn't enough that the garden looks beautiful. And it turns out that plenty of people in the world—probably the majority of the people—would agree with me. So I speak for a lot of humanity when I say that we do not feel that the beauty of a garden is enough on its own.*

Douglas Adams (if he were still alive) would probably have plenty of witty and funny things to say in response to those sorts of arguments. I don't know what he would say exactly—one of the reasons he was one of my all-time favorite writers was that he was so unpredictable—but atheists would be right to point out that even though lots of people find meaning in fairytales, some people don't seem to. And knowing the importance of the psychology of meaning to the cultural war on religion, they have started attacking Christianity on grounds that faith *inhibits* meaning and they have cast in its place an alternative, and supposedly more appealing, vision. What are we to make of the alternative vision atheists present of how to find meaning in a world comprised only of atoms?

Consider the following statement by Richard Dawkins (from his book *The Ancestor's Tale: A Pilgrimage to the Dawn of Evolution*), who is probably the best exemplar of casting this alternative vision in an attempt to appeal to the non-religious:

> *My objection to supernatural beliefs is precisely that they miserably fail to do justice to the sublime grandeur of the real world. They represent a narrowing-down from reality, an impoverishment of what the real world has to offer.*[23]

Is the atheist vision truly more expansive than Christianity? No. There is very little sense in which the Christian vision is more "narrowing" than the vision Dawkins casts. The world of the fairytale, where spirit and mind and flowers and atoms all coalesce into a vast panorama of meaning, where every stone or lake or chair may carry a message, this fairy world, which playfully combines the material and spiritual realms, is more expansive and complex than the singular flat plane of cold materialism. You may think the Christian vision wrong, and I respect that, but if you think it *narrow*, then you simply don't know what narrow means. Materialism says nothing but atoms exist.[xx] Christianity is definitely *not* narrow, whatever else it may be; it is expansive and open—it says atoms and spirits and all kinds of things that are not a part of the physical world exist.

To illustrate, let's first start with a straightforward framework for examining how narrow or expansive a belief system is. Technically speaking, a system that accepts both A and B is more expansive than a system that accepts A and *denies* B. In denying B, you are narrowing the scope of possible reality. Christianity accepts both atoms and spirit; materialist atheism denies spirit. So, Christianity is, by that framework, more expansive.

[xx] Of course, I am aware that materialism allows for those atoms to combine in ways that produce some amazing larger products – but the larger point here is that the materialist universe is (literally by definition) comprised of only material things. The Christian universe is comprised of those things, too – but it is comprised of a whole lot more.

That is not to say that the atheistic universe *on its own* ("A" in our framework) is narrow. In fact, the material universe itself is wondrously complex, so of course a universe comprised only of atoms would be wondrously complex, too. But the key point is this: Whether viewed through a Christian or a materialistic lens, the material world is still equally complicated. Both materialism *and* Christianity have no quarrel with (say) the bizarre material world of quantum physics – the Christian universe and Richard Dawkins' universe both have the same level of complexity *about material things*. (Indeed, the complexity of the material world has often been used as an argument *for* religious belief; for example, the complexity of physical life was one of the primary reasons that prominent atheist philosopher Anthony Flew changed his mind and became a theist[24]). Where we differ is that Dawkins' materialistic universe *ends* with that level of complexity, but the Christian universe adds a rather large additional layer of *spiritual* complexity. Atheist materialism is indeed complicated; but whatever complexities it has, Christianity has, too. On the other hand, Christianity's world adds on top of the material universe the beauty of the spirit, while materialism flatly denies it.

To return to our framework, if both systems fully acknowledge A, then it matters little to our larger point how complex A is. To the degree that (1) both systems have the same level of complexity about A, (2) one system acknowledges A *and* B, and (3) the other system denies B, it follows that the system that acknowledges A and B is more complex than the one that does not. The narrower system is still the one that denies B.

Is it possible that our first assumption above is wrong and Christianity has a lower level of complexity about A? Drilling down further into this argument, a materialist might object that belief in a Creator God itself is a pretty simple explanation for complex physical and psychological phenomena – and that materialism often offers much more complicated and interactive explanations. After all, "God created romantic love" sounds like a much simpler explanation than "a long history of evolutionary adaptations led to 100 billion neurons interacting in a super-complicated way, which in turn leads to a subjective experience known as falling in love."

But that argument turns out to largely be a red herring. It is based on three false assumptions. (1) First, the argument suggests that because God created X, the subsequent operation of X would somehow be simpler *merely because He created it.* There is no reason why the actual operation of romantic love would be more or less complex because God created it. Similarly, knowing God created quantum mechanics would not increase or decrease our view of its complexity.

(2) When applied to psychological phenomena, this critique also has an underlying assumption that Christians are somehow committed to the idea that psychological phenomena are not material, and that as a result we oversimplify the operations of the physical brain. I know some Christians believe such things, but I have never once been taught in any Christian context – nor do I believe – that psychological phenomena are divested of material events. I am a psychologist who believes God created our physical brain to provide physical experiences that cumulatively lead to experiences like falling in love. I have always assumed that this experience involved a wondrous, complicated set of physical events in the brain. I believe there is *more* to humanity than that – but I do not believe in *less* than the material explanation.[25]

(3) Is it possible that the backstory *origins* of phenomena are more complicated in materialist atheism than in Christianity? I do think historically Christians have often failed to embrace the possibility of scientific complexity and preferred instead to stick to simpler-sounding explanations involving God; explanations that served as a way of filling in the gaps of what we do not yet understand (see Francis Collins' book *The Language of God*[26] for an excellent discussion). Yet Christians are not committed to simple backstory explanations. Saying that "God created" something does not mean He used a simple (or complex) method to do so, any more than saying "Da Vinci created the Mona Lisa" means that Da Vinci used a simple (or complex) method of creation. In either case, it requires more information about the method itself to determine how complicated the creation process was. It is analogous to any statement where one says X caused Y: Saying "God caused" does not mean He used a simple (or complex) method of causing. If we say "God caused the Red Sea to part," there is no necessary reason to assume He used a simple method to do so – His method might have been a complicated combination of tides and wind, or it might have been as simple as *making it so* by Divine *fiat*. Either way, He

If we say "God caused the Red Sea to part," there is no necessary reason to assume He used a simple method to do so.

intervened; but as a Christian, in the grand tradition of St. Thomas Aquinas,[27] I am not specifically committed to believing in one particular method over another, and am just as open to facts that point in a complex direction as a materialist would be.

This leads me to reaffirm my original argument: It is true that atheistic materialism is complicated. But it is also true that, on balance, the Christian vision (which includes larger categories A and B) is technically more expansive than the materialist vision (which includes A and denies B).

The Subjective Psychological Argument

But technicalities aren't everything and, to be fair, I think Dawkins means "narrowing" in a more subjective psychological sense. I understand that not everyone has the same subjective experience; therefore, I can only ask the readers to make their own subjective judgments. So, consider that, in another place (his book *River Out of Eden*), Dawkins says:

> *In a universe of electrons and selfish genes, blind physical forces and genetic replication, some people are going to get hurt, other people are going to get lucky, and you won't find any rhyme or reason in it, nor any justice. The universe that we observe has precisely the properties we should expect if there is, at bottom, no design, no purpose, no evil, no good, nothing but pitiless indifference.*[28]

Now if I didn't know better, I'd say that statement could not possibly be written by the same person who spoke of doing *justice to the sublime grandeur of the real world.* I don't personally feel the sublime grandeur in the vision he casts here. I almost want to say to him: If you are genuinely inspired by a universe that has "no purpose, no evil, no good, nothing but pitiless indifference"—more power to you. But I don't feel very awe-inspired by such a description; in fact, it feels rather more like constricting my world than expanding it.

There is another sense, too, in which the atheist vision feels subjectively narrower than Christianity. Consider something Dawkins says elsewhere, in his book *Unweaving the Rainbow: Science, Delusion and the Appetite for Wonder*:

> *The feeling of awed wonder that science can give us is one of the highest experiences of which the human psyche is capable. It is a deep aesthetic passion to rank with the finest that music and poetry can deliver. It is truly one of the things that make life worth living and it does so, if anything, more effectively if it convinces us that the time we have for living is quite finite.*[29]

This vision is noble; this vision is true; this vision is beautiful. But this vision is not *expansive*. It is in fact very narrow. If you happen to like science (as I do) and are passionate enough about it to feel it does for you what music does for most people (as I am), well and good. You will get on fine with Dawkins' advice. But if you happen to think watching movies with light saber duels, or attending sporting events, or any of the other hundred things most people value more than science—if, as I say, you happen to think *those* things are awesome and science is best left to the experts, then Dawkins' narrow vision may sail by you as the proverbial ship in the night.

You may think in talking about light sabers and sports, I am providing a superficial alternative to Dawkins' vision. If you think that, it's probably because you yourself are in the category of people who passionately love science. But that love is an individual difference based on a combination of genes and opportunity; it is not a good vision for the whole human race.

Yes, it is true that a lot of people – even people who are not scientists – feel the wonder in scientific discovery. It is true that millions of people watched the moon landings, and millions more watch *NOVA* and other scientific discovery shows. But that pales in comparison to the passion people feel for Star Wars and sports. Millions of people have watched *NOVA*; but *hundreds* of millions of people have watched Star Wars.[30] Over one *hundred* million people watched the last Super Bowl.[31] And over one *billion* people watched the last World Cup soccer final.[32] And if you imagine this is just sheer numbers and the masses of people only care about those things in a superficial manner, then you clearly haven't talked to many Star Wars or sports fans, or gone to the opening day of a Star Wars movie or any major sporting event, or read many online discussions where supporters discuss their opinions about light sabers or Tom Brady with intense passion. In fact, you are wildly mistaken if you believe Star Wars and sports feel *superficial* to the people who love them.

Consider these two quotes about sports:

The game of basketball has been everything to me. My place of refuge, place I've always gone where I needed comfort and peace. It's been the site of intense pain and the most intense feelings of joy and satisfaction. It's a relationship that has evolved over time, given me the greatest respect and love for the game.[33]
Michael Jordan, Hall of Fame basketball player

Sports is the common denominator in the world that brings everyone together. If there's any one place in the world where there is equality, it is probably sports. That was something that didn't always exist. We've come a long way in sports. Why can't society use sports as a way to bring people together and create change?[34]
Stephen M. Ross, owner of the Miami Dolphins football team

Those quotes bear a striking resemblance in their approach and valence to Richard Dawkins' praise of scientific discovery. Dawkins describes science as "one of the highest experiences." In the above quotes, sports are similarly described as "everything," as a place of "refuge," as creating the "most intense feelings of joy and satisfaction," as the "only place where there is equality," and as a possible beacon of social change.

Research suggests we want other people to believe what we believe (so much so that we often imagine more people agree with us than they actually do, an effect known as the *false consensus effect*).[35] As a result, we tend to imagine that everyone either *does* or *should* value our own preferences with the same fervor we value them. Thus, the sports fan may imagine that everyone either *does* love sports as much as they do, or *should* love it as much as they do. But if you imagine, like Dawkins, that, because you love science and feel its glory, everyone else should too, then you are no different than the person who finds intense joy and satisfaction in sports and thinks everyone else should, too. That individual difference is harmless if that's as far as it goes – but it is *not* harmless to build a vision for the human race out of one's own personal preference for science or sports. Yes, discovering scientific facts is awesome and that curiosity is a big part of what makes us human; but the lessons learned in sports are also awesome and no less a part of what makes us human. And Star Wars was so inspiring to so many people that it literally caused the formation of a new religion based on the movie – a religion that is the largest "alternative" religion in the United Kingdom according to official census data (with over 170,000 adherents)[36] and for which thousands of students on a Turkish college campus signed a petition to create a religious temple.[37]

The larger point is this: It is tempting to dismiss the individual variability in the relative value people place on science versus other things and suggest the flaw is with *those people* who do not "get" science. After all, Dawkins says that it is *a deep aesthetic passion to rank with the finest that music and poetry can deliver.* Dawkins of course does not suggest the fault lies with the masses, but one wonders – if this is the vision we are supposed to adhere to – what the person does who cannot feel this passion, either because they are not built that way or because their life does not provide the opportunity?

Christianity casts rather a wider net. The Bible says that all good things were made by God for us to enjoy (1 Timothy 6:17). The passion for scientific discovery is wonderful, but it is not ascribed a higher value than the passion for sports. Christianity does not say to you "if you don't feel awe and wonder the way scientists feel it about quantum physics, then you will not experience one of the highest experiences the human psyche can experience. Sorry about that." Rather, it says "a life can have sublime meaning even if you have no interest in quantum mechanics or biology—you can experience joy and peace and awe and wonder, even if you don't have the desire or opportunity to experience it in that particular way."

Of course, Dawkins (nor no atheist that I know) is arguing that science is the only passion that matters. I do not know Dawkins, but his own writings clearly suggest he values music and poetry and plenty of other things beyond science. And I do know many materialist atheists personally and none of them believe that science is the only valuable human experience. But here I am only addressing the narrowness or expansiveness of the vision that Dawkins – arguably the most famous atheist apologist of the last 30 years – himself casts. When pushed for what his vision is, he argues for the glory of science to be central. And my point is this: That vision may be many things, but choosing one possible meaningful experience out of a thousand and making that experience the primary one that matters is not *expansive.*

Now, I happen to agree with him about the sublime beauty of science. In *his* world, I'm one of the lucky ones. I have a deep aesthetic passion for science, too. I believe it is better than poetry (a low bar, in my opinion) and on par with music (one of the highest bars imaginable). But if the alternative vision presented by atheists involves replacing the awe of fairyland with the awe of science—well, I feel bad for anyone who does not feel quite the wonder of science that Dawkins feels. Christianity's expansive and complex vision allows for *all* kinds of people to experience it. It gives the same chance to the poor and uneducated as to the rich and well-to-do. Christ does not require you to be Richard Dawkins or Stephen Hawking to invite you into His story.

It is also worth remembering that Dawkins asserts that my belief system "*miserably fail[s] to do justice to the sublime grandeur of the real world*" and "*represent[s] a narrowing-down from reality, an impoverishment of what the real world has to offer.*" But this is patently false in my experience. Being a Christian has not, not for one solitary second, meant I have missed out on the intense awe of studying the natural world. I experience that awe, but I experience a lot *more* than that. If Christianity is true, then awe is available to *everybody everywhere* in a way that doesn't require them to understand science in order to feel alive. If I wasn't a scientist and didn't feel the sublime beauty of an atom or a quasar or a neuron, if I wasn't hungry for knowledge of thermodynamics or the hypothalamus—if, in short, I did not feel the beauty in the drive to understand the natural world through science that Dawkins describes—I would still be able to live a life worth living. I don't think Dawkins would say my life would be *meaningless* if I didn't value scientific discovery, but he does pitch an alternative vision that places a very high value on it. I find that vision subjectively narrowing.[xxi]

[xxi] Applying these same thoughts to the arguments of this chapter, it is of course possible that these tables could be turned by arguing that I am over-valuing the importance of *religious* experience. Is it fair to say I am taking that one part of human experience and turning that *religious* part into the *whole shebang*? On the one hand, it is almost certainly the case that I over-estimate religion's psychological importance to the average person, and, aware of that possibility, I have tried to be careful to qualify that argument in this chapter. However, I do not think the *Christian framework* and Dawkins' *science framework* are actually in quite the same relationship to other human experiences. Christianity teaches that all good things come from God and thus provides an overarching lens by which to assign value to *all* varied good human experiences. However, in trying to substitute science for religion, it is unclear to me that the drive for scientific discovery has quite the same overarching scope. One can of course see that the joy of scientific discovery is a part of many things – for example, Star Wars is a form of *science* fiction – but I do not think the glorious experience of sitting by the fire with my family, or the joy in watching a Montana snowfall, or the wonder

So, while I realize some people do not experience the aching for a better world in a lonely sunset, or feel the voice of God calling in a thunderstorm (and I rarely experience those things myself)—nonetheless, the Christian vision explicitly endorses a larger variety of psychological experience. And my human machine has always benefitted from the fairy-tale-meets-facts Christian worldview.

Concluding Thoughts: Getting Behind a Meaningful Life

The danger of this chapter is to sound as if I'm claiming atheists don't have meaningful lives because they only believe in atoms. Let me be clear—I don't mean that at all. I know many atheists and most of them are wonderful friends, parents, and colleagues. They view their lives as meaningful and so do I.

Rather, my purpose is to examine the kind of psychology that makes the human machine run best. Atheists attack Christianity on the grounds that we *ruin* meaning, claiming humanity would be better off if we could only lose our archaic and simple-minded view that there is something in this world besides atoms. However, the evidence suggests they are wrong. The Christian view of meaning isn't simple-minded at all. It is an expansive and complex vision where atoms and fairytales meet, where the earth-plow meets prayer. Materialism alone will likely never satisfy this desire for both atoms *and* spirit. But Christianity provides a roadmap that matches this complicated psychological landscape.

---

of sharing a football game with 25,000 other people, are *possibly* related directly to scientific discovery in the same way that my religion is related to those things for me. That is not to say atheists do not experience those things – but only that I do not think substituting their vision of those things for the Christian vision is subjectively more expansive.

CHAPTER SIX
OBJECTIVITY MEETS INTIMACY: THE PSYCHOLOGY OF GOD

The God of the Old Testament is arguably the most unpleasant character in all fiction: jealous and proud of it; a petty, unjust, unforgiving control-freak; a vindictive, bloodthirsty ethnic cleanser; a misogynistic, homophobic, racist, infanticidal, genocidal, filicidal, pestilential, megalomaniacal, sadomasochistic, capriciously malevolent bully.
Richard Dawkins[1]

Who needs Satan when you have a God like this?
Robert M. Price[2]

God is a comedian playing to an audience too afraid to laugh.
Voltaire[3]

Why should I allow that same God to tell me how to raise my kids, who had to drown His own?
Robert G. Ingersoll[4]

Men rarely (if ever) manage to dream up a God superior to themselves. Most Gods have the manners and morals of a spoiled child.
Robert A Heinlein, from *The Atheist's Bible*[5]

If you compare what atheists say about the Biblical picture of God and what Christians say about that same picture, you might not believe the two groups were reading the same book. Christians routinely glory in God's amazing love and patience. By contrast, as suggested by the above quotes, a lot of atheists don't even *like* God—especially the Christian God. They think he is mean-spirited and angry; they think he is an egoist; they think all sorts of nasty things about Him.

I have some empathy with the atheists; I don't always *like* God either. I'm not alone. Indeed, most people who come to the Bible for the first time to seriously study the character of God are surprised—and sometimes appalled—by what they find. That includes famous

Christian converts such as C.S. Lewis, who once wrote in a letter to a former student: "Everyone told me that [in the Gospels] I should find a figure who I couldn't help loving. Well, I could." He later elaborates: "The first thing you find is that we are simply not *invited* to speak, to pass any moral judgment on Him, however favorable; it is only too clear that He is going to be doing whatever judging there is…[T]here is a good deal in the character which, unless He really is what He says he is, is not lovable or even tolerable."[6]

So I feel like I am in good company when I say that sometimes the picture of God in the Bible (and especially, but not limited to, the Old Testament) alarms me and disturbs me. I do not lightly dismiss—nor should you—the accusations atheists hurl at God.

Often this debate is cast under the rubric of the problem of evil—but that's not what I am talking about. I do not claim to have a good solution to the philosophical problem of evil. Other and smarter minds have discussed that issue until I'm not sure much more can be said about it.

And indeed, I am not much troubled by the *philosophical problem* of evil—but *actual evil*. Stuff happens to me in my life and I don't know why—*that* troubles me. And when it seems the character of God in the Bible isn't very *good*, that troubles me also.

And yet—I believe in the Biblical God. My reasons for believing in Him are complex and multi-faceted, but in this chapter I'm going to tackle some of the issues relevant to the difficult issues involved in how God is pictured in the Bible.

Since the picture of the Christian God in the Bible is one of the things atheists frequently use against Christianity, it's important to spend some time offering a different view of God than that of a spoiled, poorly-mannered child or a malevolent bully. I have read the Christian Creeds and Scriptures—and while I certainly can see why the atheists say what they say, nonetheless I feel very differently about the larger picture that emerges from the Biblical narratives.

In this chapter, we focus first on some broad brushstrokes that emerge from traditional Christian view of God. While I do not pretend the emerging picture deals with, say, the problem of why God seems to orchestrate some terrible things in the Old Testament, I do think it deals with some of the issues atheists have expressed (and humanity has expressed) concerning why they don't seem to *like* God. Part of it is that we need to more fully and deeply grasp that something can be *both* distant *and* close—and this is what we turn to next.

Keeping Both Sides of God

Your god is too small for my universe.
Carl Sagan[7]

In this spirit, it seems to me that if the word "God" is to be of any use, it should be taken to mean an interested God, a creator and lawgiver who has established not only the laws of nature and the universe but also standards of good and evil, some personality that is concerned with our actions, something in short that is appropriate for us to worship. That is the God that has mattered to men and women throughout history.... If there is a God that has special plans for humans, then He has taken very great pains to hide His concern for us.
Steven Weinberg, Nobel-Prize winning scientist and atheist[8]

Carl Sagan suggests that the typical picture of God is too *local* or *quaint* to fit the bigness of things. On the other hand, Steven Weinberg suggests God is not quite local *enough*—that He isn't quite present enough here on earth. Both types of complaints are ubiquitous, and not just amongst atheists. I know of few honest Christians who would claim they have never felt God's absence. I know of few honest Christians who would claim they have never felt God was too small to handle their problems.

I am not trying to explain away all your personal experiences, good and bad. I am asking you to reflect on the psychology of what you'd expect God to *be like*. The picture of God that emerges from Christian teaching is a sweeping vision that paints Him as simultaneously bigger than Carl Sagan's universe *and* more locally present than Steven Weinberg could ever envision. It seems to me that many errors about what God is like have emerged from having a too-simple view of God that leaves out one side of this equation.

There is a sense that Christian doctrine exists to balance various truths, but it is important to define what we mean by *balance*. Sometimes, that balance means something more like *compromise*. Compromise is finding a middle path between two points, as when you want the price to be $100 and I want it to be $50, and so we agree on $75.

Many errors about what God is like have emerged from having a too-simple view of God.

Although Christian doctrine is not entirely devoid of that kind of balance, nonetheless Christianity generally does not offer a compromise between two points as a solution for the tension between them. When Christianity teaches you should show *justice* to the criminal but also says you should be *compassionate* to the same criminal, one may wonder how to act when it appears those two things are in conflict. But, whatever else Christianity means about balancing justice and compassion, it doesn't in any way mean you should be *sort of* just and *sort of* compassionate. It also doesn't mean you should be just to one criminal and compassionate to another. Instead, it most definitely asserts that you should be *completely* just and *completely* compassionate, at the same time, to all criminals you encounter.

I said Christian doctrine provides *balance* in these cases, but that isn't quite the right word, either. A better word would be *combination.* Christianity doesn't merely *balance* mercy and compassion, as a judge might weigh leniency for the criminal with consideration of the victim, and find some kind of compromise; instead, it *combines* compassion and justice. It makes them both happen at the same time, all the while keeping them both *in their full glory*. These standards do not become less themselves for being combined with each other; in fact, compassion becomes more compassionate, and justice more just, for operating together.

It probably goes without saying that this approach is complex. So it is. Taking two seemingly unlike things and weaving them into a larger tapestry is the very definition of the highest levels of complexity.[9] Imagine two metal sculptures, one of a swan and one of a flute. It is not very complex to melt the two structures down into a singular metal blob. But it is the height of complexity to keep the swan and the flute, but weave them into a larger sculpture where both their swan-ness and their flute-ness are still evident. They are woven together, and yet in the very act of weaving, their own natures become more (not less) evident. Indeed, by juxtaposing two, so seemingly different entities—one an animal, one a man-made instrument—the shared qualities of both become poetically apparent. We suddenly see the gracefulness of the swan and the gracefulness of the flute's music as shared qualities. The very act of contrasting illuminates

They are woven together, and yet in the very act of weaving, their own natures become more (not less) evident.

those qualities that can be compared—which, in turn, reinforces the qualities of the entities as individuals.

Christian doctrine often attempts such a feat: It attempts to keep two positive things as wholly themselves, and yet weaves them together. The topic of this chapter is one such case: Is God close to us or far away? Christianity argues that God is both wholly other from us, and yet infinitely close to us. As such, it is unsurprising that God is depicted as being angry at people when they hurt each other, and it is also unsurprising that He is depicted as being incredibly compassionate to people who do the hurting.

God is Both Separate and Reachable

We have a tendency as humans to take one truth and act like it is the only thing in the entire universe. After all, when I find a bowl of raw cookie dough calling to me like a long-lost friend, it has a way of gripping my attention, causing other facts to fade into the background. Christian doctrine helps correct this human tendency. It helps us avoid focusing on one of God's characteristics and assuming that is the *only* thing about Him that matters. Thus, we spend time below discussion both sides of the Biblical picture of God.

God is Wholly Separate…

We are speaking of God, what marvel if thou do not comprehend? For if thou comprehend, He is not God.
St. Augustine, *Confessions*[10]

He cannot be seen—He is brighter than light. Nor can He be grasped—He is purer than touch. He cannot be estimated, for He is greater than all perceptions. He is infinite and immense. His greatness is known to Himself alone.
Mark Minucius Felix[11]

I believe in God the Father, Almighty Maker of heaven and earth.
Nicene Creed[12,13]

The Bible says in Ephesians 4:6 that God is "over all and through all and in all." From that and other similar verses, one might imagine

Christianity teaches – as some pantheistic religions do – that God basically *is* everything. That He *is* the rock, the tree, and – that God is *us*.

Yet, Christianity also teaches that God is set apart from us, holy, vast beyond measure, infinite and uncontrollable in ways we cannot fully understand. This theme is evident throughout the Bible. Isaiah 46:5 says: "To whom will you compare me or count me equal?" (46:5). A little later in Isaiah, this theme is echoed: "I am God, and there is no other; I am God, and there is none like me" (46:9). Given that Christians view of God as Creator of everyone and everything, it is unsurprising that we view Him as completely *other* from us. As it says in Acts (17:25): "He is not served by human hands, as if He needed anything, because he himself gives all men life and breath and everything else" (Acts 17:25). But God isn't just bigger and stronger than us: It is made clear in multiple places that this applies to moral superiority, too, as in Numbers 23:19: "God is not human, that he should lie, not a human being, that he should change his mind."

This sense of otherness is probably never more evident than in the last five chapters of the book of Job. In that book, Job spends quite a long time – nearly 37 chapters – challenging God's wisdom and sovereignty. And at the end of the book, God answers Job's challenge. God's response is not quite what I would have predicted; it is a very long set of sweeping questions designed to illustrate that God and Job are not in the same category. Here is but a very small sampling of those questions that God posed to Job: "Where were you when I laid the earth's foundation?" (Job 38:4). "Have you ever given orders to the morning, or shown the dawn its place?" (Job 38:12). "Have the gates of death been shown to you? Have you seen the gates of the deepest darkness?" (38:17). "Can you raise your voice to the clouds and cover yourself with a flood of water?" "Do you send the lightning bolts on their way? Do they report to you and say 'here we are'?" (38:34-35). By the end of the book, there is no doubt: God is completely and wholly *other* than Job – or anyone else.

Thus, Christianity flatly denies the conflation of God and his creation. It is in direct contradiction with the doctrine that God is wholly *other*. So whatever else Christianity means by saying that God is "*in* all," it doesn't mean that He *is* all. Rather,

Christianity flatly denies the conflation of God and his creation.

He is the *Maker* of everything. In Isaiah 44:19-20, God addresses persons who make idols out of a block of wood: "No one stops to think, no one has knowledge or understanding to say, 'Half of it I used for fuel; I even baked bread over its coals, I roasted meat and I ate. Shall I make a detestable thing from what is left? Shall I bow down to a block of wood' Such a person feeds on ashes; a deluded heart misleads him; he cannot save himself, or say 'Is not this thing in my right hand a lie?'" Thus, God specifically denies that He is a part of creation or can be equated to it. It is the difference between believing God is the paint in the painting and believing God is the *Painter.* The sense in which He is *in everything* is more like the sense that a painter's touch and love is everywhere present in his painting, but He is not the paint itself.

...And Yet He is Reachable

I am His daughter, He said so. Oh, infinite gentleness of God!
Oh, word so long desired, so urgently besought! Ocean of joy!
'My daughter!"
St. Margaret of Cortona[14]

The air is in the sunshine and the sunshine in the air.
So likewise is God in the being of the soul.
Bl. Jan van Ruysbroeck[15]

Therese had simply disappeared, like a drop lost in the ocean.
Jesus only was left, my Master, my King.
St. Therese de Lisieux[16]

Out of love the Lord took us to Himself.
Clement of Rome[17]

Who, for us and for our salvation, came down from Heaven.
Nicene Creed[18]

On the other side of the canyon, there is an equally dangerous error: To believe God is *unreachable.* Given that Christianity teaches that God is so completely different, it might be easy to believe He is an objective judge who is too distant from us to be reached in any meaningful way.

But this perception is also contradicted directly by Christian teachings. The Nicene Creed states: "Who, for us and for our salvation, *came down from Heaven…*" God is *with us*. This theme is carried throughout the Bible. Consider just a small sampling of versus that directly state God's intense desire to be close to us. Jesus (who is, in Christian theology, the perfect representation of God on earth) says to His disciples in John 14:3-4 (emphasis mine in all cases in this section): "And if I go and prepare a place for you, I will come back and take you with me that *you also may be where I am*." He also tells them at a later point "*I am with you* always, even to the end of the age" (Matthew 28:20). Indeed, in the Bible, the human story opens in a world where God walks with Adam and Eve in the Garden (Genesis 3:8) and ends with God again directly with His people: "Then I saw a new heaven and a new earth….and there was longer any sea…And I heard a loud voice from the throne, saying 'Now the dwelling of God is with men, and He will live with them. They will be His people, and God Himself with *be with them* and be their God" (Revelation 21:1-3).

Given that Christianity teaches that God is so completely different, it might be easy to believe He is an objective judge who is too distant from us to be reached in any meaningful way.

But the God of the Bible doesn't just want to *hang out in the general vicinity of* humans in a casual, don't-get-to-close-to-me kind of way. Rather, He wants to be *extremely* intimate with us. How close? He wants to live *inside* of us. Jesus says in John 14:23 that "My Father will love them, and we will come to them and *make our home with them*." He isn't just going to be a casual passerby – He's going to live *with* us, *in* us. In fact, the Bible is replete with images of God's expressions of desired intimacy with His creation. Some of that language is almost shocking in its relational intimacy: We are "adopted as children" (Romans 8:23; Ephesians 1:5; Galatians 4:1-7) and called "friends" of God (John 15:15). Indeed, sometimes the Biblical metaphors are so bracing in expressions of intimacy that, were they not in the Bible, I might find them blasphemous: For example, our relationship to God is compared to a romantic marriage relationship, as when we are repeatedly called the "bride" of God and Him a "bridegroom" (Isaiah 62:4-5; Matthew

25:1-5; Mark 2:19; Ephesians 5:31-32; Revelation 19:7; Revelation 21:9; Revelation 22:17; Revelation 21:2-3).

God is *not* us – He is other. The painter isn't the paint. Yet Christianity teaches that He cared so much about His creation that He came down into it; He condescended to *take on* its form in this unfathomable way (Philippians 2:6), to be as close to us as He could.

God cared so much about His creation that He came down into it.

It matters not which side of the canyon you fall off; it'll hurt just the same. Believing God is *only* the paint is not very functional, but believing God is nowhere to be found in His own painting is worse still. Christian doctrine exists in part to counteract both of these wrong views of God by keeping each view wholly in mind at all times, and thus *compromising neither view.* God isn't the same as us, but He isn't absent from us, either. He isn't the rock you can reach down and pick up with your hand, but He is *reachable* all the same. In fact, Christianity teaches that He came to Earth to reach you.

Reconciling Otherness and Nearness: Justice Meets Compassion

Invisible in his own nature he became visible in ours. Beyond our grasp, he chose to come within our grasp. Existing before time began, he began to exist at a moment in time. Incapable of suffering as God, he did not refuse to be a man, capable of suffering. Immortal, he chose to be subject to the laws of death.
Leo the Great[19]

This morning my soul is greater than the world since it possesses You, You Whom heaven and earth do not contain.
St. Margaret of Cortona[20]

In his recent book "Against Empathy," Yale psychology professor Paul Bloom argues that empathy – having emotional compassion for others – is a "poor moral guide."[21] Why? Because it can affect our ability to be *fair.* According to Bloom, empathy leads to "favoring the one over the many."[22] Empathy thus interferes with justice. Imagine a murderer who was tragically orphaned as a young child and abused by a series of foster parents. If a judge feels empathy towards the difficult circumstances of the murderer, the judge might neglect to consider both the family of the victim *and* the potential threat to society at large. Indeed, in research on empathy, having someone remain an "objective judge" systematically reduces their empathy for the one they are judging.[23]

The Angry Justice of God

As Bloom's book suggests,[24] people value fairness; and Christian doctrine unambiguously and repeatedly reveals that God is completely fair. In Acts 10:34-35, the Bible says: "Then Peter began to speak: 'I now realize how true it is that God does not show favoritism, but accepts from every nation the one who fears him and does what is right.'"[xxii] As such, God is depicted as the ultimate arbiter of justice across all people. If people do things wrong, He will judge them with perfect fairness. Murder, for example, demands some kind of justice. People cannot forever be allowed to go on murdering; they must be punished for their crimes. Who would want to live in a universe that was wholly unjust, where everyone fared alike no matter what they did?

People in our culture value fairness; but it seems like they do not value *anger*. I think our culture's sentiment about anger is captured in the philosophy of the beloved Star Wars character Yoda: *Anger is a path to the dark side*. This theme is echoed in many atheists' modern attacks on Christian belief. They often throw around accusations regarding God's anger as if it makes him *bad*. "Good heavens," they seem to cry, "if you only knew about that intense anger, you would be horrified and leave your faith." For example, In Dan Barker's book *God: The Most Unpleasant Character in All Fiction*, he spends quite a bit of time attacking God's character using examples from the Bible that focus on how *angry* God seems.[25] As an exemplar, Barker claims God is mean-spirited

---

[xxii] There are certainly instances in the Bible where it appears to me that God is not being fair. The point of this section is not to suggest everything God does in the Bible will seem obviously fair at first reading. It is rather to suggest that the Bible repeatedly asserts in the abstract that God is in fact fair and just. As a Christian, I have come to trust that instances where it appears to me God is unfair would be analogous to hearing about a judge's decision that seemed unfair to me where I did not have all the evidence. *If I trust the judge*, I would trust that, were it possible for me to know everything the judge knows, I would deem the decision fair.

because God says in Ezekiel 7:8-9: "I am about to pour out my wrath on you and spend my anger against you. I will judge you according to your conduct and repay you for all your detestable practices. I will not look on you with pity; I will not spare you."

There is no denying God is often depicted as angry in the Bible, and some of this language is intense and hard to stomach. Often, His anger is connected to His sense of justice; and thus His anger is directed at sinners doing wrong things. For example, Romans 2:5 says "But because of your stubbornness and your unrepentant heart, you are storing up wrath against yourself for the day of God's wrath, when his righteous judgment will be revealed." We often balk at such language. "God's wrath?" "Righteous judgment?" These words often make God sound to the modern ear like an angry dictator who is on an ego trip, not like a patient judge distributing justice.

But that sentiment sometimes does not take into account exactly what God is mad *about.* He is often angry because people are severely hurt by sin. "Justice" isn't just an abstract concept in the Bible – it involves considering the horrible consequences of sin for the people who are hurt by it. We develop this concept a little later in this chapter, but here I would like to note this: Plenty of things about the Bible trouble me, but God's intense anger at sin and injustice is not one of them.[xxiii] Quite the contrary: I would hope God *would* be angry at someone who tried to (say) murder my daughter. I wouldn't find a lack of anger in that sense to be *good*; I would find it to be *apathetic.* Indifference to horrible crimes seems itself horrible to me. I prefer a God who is emotionally invested in wanting justice. My attitude is often like that of Calvin in Bill Watterson's famous *Calvin and Hobbes* cartoon (curiously quoted in *The Atheist's Bible*[26]): "It's hard to be religious when certain people are never incinerated by bolts of lightning."

Indifference to horrible crimes seems itself horrible to me.

[xxiii] As Barker notes, much of God's anger in the Bible does not seem clearly directed at justice to other people; for example, quite a bit of it is about worshipping other gods. This appears narcissistic to Barker and to others – and sometimes to me, too. I do not dismiss these passages lightly, although I would interpret many of them differently (since the Bible also directly equates our worship of God to our treatment of other people, I view those two kinds of commands through the same lens). Nonetheless, the purpose of this chapter is to provide a framework for considering the psychology of our view of God, and as such, considering one streamlined example that often troubles people is a useful starting point.

The Compassionate Empathy of God

In practical reality, empathy may sometimes interfere with justice (as Bloom notes in his book). But that does not mean empathy itself is *bad.* In fact, being empathic is generally held in high esteem by most people. And for good reason: Empathy is one of the best predictors of clearly good behaviors. As one example, consider a famous psychology study.[27] All participants listened to a radio show where they heard about a fellow student ("Carol") who had been in an accident, was having some medical problems, and was in need of a tutor in the very class the participants themselves were in. Some of the participants had been told before the show to listen with an "objective" mindset that kept them at a distance from Carol; others had been told to listen with an "empathic" mindset that would allow them to be emotionally close to Carol. Those who listened with an objective mindset volunteered to help Carol when it would make them feel personally better to do so; but they did not volunteer to help her much at all when they could feel better some other way. However, participants with an empathic mindset helped her almost all of the time regardless of the degree to which it would impact their own personal feelings. Removing empathy can make you more objectively fair; but it can also make you more selfish. Increasing empathy increases the chance you will selflessly help across multiple contexts.

In line with the positive value of empathy, God is consistently described in the Bible as empathic. We have already discussed the Biblical expressions of God's closeness to us, but other Bible verses show clearly that God *feels emotionally* for our lives, our trials, and our pain. The word "empathy" itself does not appear in modern translations of the Bible, but many similarly emotive words are ascribed to God throughout the Bible. For example, God is often called by a synonym of empathic[28]: "compassionate." Exodus 22:26-27 says: "If you take your neighbor's cloak as a pledge, return it by sunset, because that cloak is the only covering your neighbor has. What else can they sleep in? When they cry out to me, I will hear, for I am compassionate." This *God is compassionate* theme is carried throughout the Bible, including the description of the father (God) in

Removing empathy can make you more objectively fair; but it can also make you more selfish.

the famous parable of the prodigal son: "But while he was still a long way off, his father saw him and was filled with compassion for him; he ran to his son, threw his arms around him and kissed him" (Luke 15:20). Isaiah 49:15-16 echoes this sentiment, with God expressing tender emotion towards His children: "Can a mother forget the baby at her breast and have no compassion on the child she has borne? Though she may forget, I will not forget you! See, I have engraved you on the palms of my hands."

Even when the word "compassion" is not used, the Bible clearly depicts God as caring deeply about our feelings and circumstances in an intimately emotional way. For example, Psalm 34:18 says: "The Lord is near to the brokenhearted and saves the crushed in spirit." Elsewhere, we are told not to worry because God knows our needs (Luke 12:30), that He cares about our anxieties (1 Peter 5:7), and that he understands the trials and temptations we face (Hebrews 2:18, 1 Corinthians 10:13). The spirit of these verses is summed up in Jesus' famous pronouncement in Matthew 11: 28-29: "Come to me, all you who are weary and burdened, and I will give you rest. Take my yoke upon you and learn from me, for I am gentle and humble in heart, and you will find rest for your souls." God cares about and understands our burdens.

The Bible clearly depicts God as caring deeply about our feelings and circumstances in an intimately emotional way.

Justice is Empathy for the Victim

At the outset of this chapter, I said Christian teaching often combines two sides of a particular psychological tension, and in so doing, it keeps both sides in all their original beauty. Perhaps nowhere is that more evident than in the case of justice and empathy. The intertwining of empathy and justice can be seen in at least two different ways.

First, the Bible recognizes the important fact that part of justice is empathy for the *victim*. Indeed, it is rather remarkable how often the Bible talks about compassion and justice in the same breath. Consider the following verses:

Therefore the Lord waits to be gracious to you, and therefore he exalts himself to show mercy to you. For the Lord is a God of justice; blessed are all those who wait for him. For a people shall dwell in Zion, in Jerusalem; you shall weep no more. He will surely be gracious to you at the sound of your cry. As soon as he hears it, he answers you (Isaiah 30:18-19).

Turn away from evil and do good; so shall you dwell forever. For the Lord loves justice; he will not forsake his saints. They are preserved forever, but the children of the wicked shall be cut off (Psalm 37:29).

Learn to do right; seek justice. Defend the oppressed. Take up the cause of the fatherless; plead the case of the widow (Isaiah 1:17).

He executes justice for the fatherless and the widow, and loves the sojourner, giving him food and clothing (Deuteronomy 10:18).

Open your mouth for the mute, for the rights of all who are destitute. Open your mouth, judge righteously, defend the rights of the poor and needy (Proverbs 31: 8-9).

Then I will draw near to you for judgment. I will be a swift witness against the sorcerers, against the adulterers, against those who swear falsely, against those who oppress the hired worker in his wages, the widow and the fatherless, against those who thrust aside the sojourner, and do not fear me, says the Lord of hosts (Malachi 3:5).

In these verses, not only is judgment paired with compassion rhetorically, in many cases judgment is *driven* by compassion. God executes justice *for* the oppressed, *for* the fatherless, *for* the widow, as a result His compassion. His justice exists because he will not forsake his saints – that is, justice exists on their behalf. Thus, it is important to note that God's justice meets His empathy in part because perfect empathy for everyone would *inspire* justice.

Justice and Empathy on the Cross

The LORD is compassionate and gracious, slow to anger, abounding in love. He will not always accuse, nor will he harbor his anger forever; he does not treat us as our sins deserve or repay us according to our iniquities. For as high as the heavens are above the earth, so great is his love for those who fear him; as far as the east is from the west, so far has he removed our transgressions from us. As a father has compassion on his children, so the LORD has compassion on those who fear him (Psalm 103: 8-13).

Of course, while empathy for the victim is clearly related to justice for the victim, that still leaves us with a puzzle: We are all perpetrators of bad actions that have hurt other people. Yes, I want God to be mad at someone who tried to kill my daughter. But how can His perfect justice be implemented given the fact that, as it says in Romans 3:23, "All have sinned and fallen short of the glory of God"? We are all worthy of punishment. Given that, isn't God in a bit of a dilemma here? Because if he (to quote from the above Psalm) "does not treat us as our sins deserve," isn't He violating His own sense of justice?

It is a fundamental part of Christian belief that Jesus died on a cross for our sins. It turns out that it is hard to state Christian doctrine about the meaning of the cross without becoming complex on the spot. For the cross is indeed a kind of psychological cross-roads: It is the meeting of God's justice and God's empathy. Those two things collide on the cross. God knows we all deserve death[xxiv]—justice. But God is too close to us to *want* us to die, and desires to give us a second chance we do not deserve—mercy. The cross accomplishes both, because God *stands in our place.* He Himself takes the justice we deserve. A penalty must be meted: He takes it upon Himself.

For the cross is indeed a kind of psychological cross-roads: It is the meeting of God's justice and God's empathy. Those two things collide on the cross.

[xxiv] Part of our own misunderstanding of God's wrath is that we fail to apply the oft-repeated Christian mantra "love the sinner, hate the sin" to ourselves. God is always, in a sense, angry at my own sin. My own redemption started with recognizing that, for all time, God is *right* to be angry at it. I hurt people and that's bad – and God will never be "ok" with my sin at any point in His existence. What had to change wasn't His wrath, but my acknowledgment that He is right to be wrathful. When I look back at my own sin, I am now angry at myself for doing it and recognize that my sin really *did* deserve punishment by death. But I also know that I have been forgiven for it on the Cross – that Lucian Conway, the sinner, has been spared the rich punishment that my sin warranted. That said, I do realize that this issue itself can be complicated and I have written about it on my blog more extensively than we have space for here.

Consider the following discussions of this doctrine in the Bible:

> *When they hurled their insults at him, he did not retaliate; when he suffered, he made no threats. Instead, he entrusted himself to him who judges justly. "He himself bore our sins" in his body on the cross, so that we might die to sins and live for righteousness; "by his wounds you have been healed" (1 Peter 2:23-34).*
>
> *When you were dead in your sins and in the uncircumcision of your flesh, God made you alive with Christ. He forgave us all our sins, having canceled the charge of our legal indebtedness, which stood against us and condemned us; he has taken it away, nailing it to the cross (Colossians 2:13-14).*
>
> *For God was pleased to have all his fullness dwell in him, and through him to reconcile to himself all things, whether things on earth or things in heaven, by making peace through his blood, shed on the cross. Once you were alienated from God and were enemies in your minds because of your evil behavior. But now he has reconciled you by Christ's physical body through death to present you holy in his sight, without blemish and free from accusation (Colossians 1:19-21).*
>
> *...God was reconciling the world to Himself through Christ, not counting people's sins against them (2 Corinthians 4:3).*

As evident in these verses, in Christianity, the Cross is the crossroads of justice and empathy. God *reconciled* Himself to us there – that is, he become close to us. But He felt so strongly about justice that to accomplish this reconciliation in full, He literally had to take on human form and die.

This bold Christian doctrine combines the emotional nearness of God (that is, His empathetic closeness to us) with the shocking moral otherness of God (that is, His moral distance from us). What Christianity says, in stark contrast to many belief systems, is that *both* of these things are true about God. God is *wholly* just, but He is also *wholly* compassionate.

Interestingly, atheists sometimes attack this very resolution as a slight against God's character. In the forward to Dan Barker's book *God: The Most Unpleasant Character in All Fiction*, Richard Dawkins says[29]: "There's little in the Old Testament to match the horror of St. Paul's version of the ancient principle of the scapegoat: The Creator of the Universe and Inventor of the Laws of Physics couldn't think of a better way to forgive our sins (especially the sin of Adam, who never existed and therefore never sinned) than to have himself hideously tortured and executed in human form as vicarious punishment. As Paul's Epistle to the Hebrews (9:22) puts it, 'without the shedding of blood there is no forgiveness.'"

I can understand the sentiment and have elaborated on this argument on my blog.[30] And yet, I think the sentiment itself is based on the assumption that my own sin does not deserve serious wrath. I cannot speak for Richard Dawkins' sin; but I am completely convinced that my own sin is, in fact, worthy of death. And therefore I find it rather strange – given that fact – to imagine, as Richard Dawkins does, that God's willingness to *take my place* and endure torture and death on my behalf makes Him such a monster. Quite the contrary – I rather feel immense gratitude for His sacrifice on my behalf.

Concluding Thoughts

"The Lady of Lorien! Galadriel!" cried Sam." You should see her, indeed you should, sir. Beautiful she is, sir! Lovely! Sometimes like a great tree in flower, sometimes like a white daffadowndilly, small and slender like. Hard as di'monds, soft as moonlight. Warm as sunlight, cold as frost in the stars. Proud and far-off as a snow-mountain, and as merry as any lass I ever saw with daisies in her hair in springtime. But that's a lot 'o nonsense, and all wide of my mark."

"Then she must be lovely indeed," said Faramir. "Perilously fair."
From J.R.R. Tolkien's *The Lord of the Rings*[31]

It is practically a part of the human condition that persons desire both intimacy and objectivity. Everyone, everywhere desires belongingness, the companionship of others, to be understood, to be known.[32] There is no corner of the globe where people do not wish their names to be known, the hairs on their heads to be numbered. Intimacy.

Everyone, everywhere desires fairness. The rule of reciprocity—that is, if someone does something to you, you should do it in return—is one of the few human norms that seem pervasive across *all* cultures.[33] There is nowhere on earth where people do not desire fairness and justice. Objectivity.

Yet people sometimes desire these things in different degrees. And that's ok. The Bible teaches that God *made* people to be different, a point we return to in Chapter 7. Some people strongly desire God's amazing *nearness*: They want to lay shamelessly in His compassionate arms, hope to see His tenderness in every rock, every stream, every baby's cry. But other people are struck by God's remarkable *otherness*: They want to stand in awe of the fact that He is separate, perfect, holy, and unlike anything else that ever existed. Christianity embraces *both* of those things, rightly understood, yet it also warns against believing one without the other. In other words, it warns against a too-simple view of God.

To the person who revels in God's *nearness,* Christianity teaches something like this:

> *God is near; God loves you; He wants you to feel His love in every rock and stream and baby's cry, because that's exactly why He made those things; that is the Truth. But do not imagine that because God desires nearness to you more than anything, that He is less omnipotent or perfect or mighty or strong. Do not imagine that because God desires union with humanity that He* is *humanity. He will always be untamable and wholly God.*

To the person who revels in God's *otherness*, Christianity teaches something like this:

> *God is wholly other; God is indeed perfect; he is indeed unlike anything else in the universe. He made all and no one else could have ever done such marvelous deeds. He alone knows all and can do all. But do not imagine that, because God is different from everything, He is distant from everything. God is as close to you as a breathed prayer at every moment of your life; and never forget that the Bible says He wants to be in union with you, yes, even as a bride to a bridegroom.*

Christianity meets these twin complex desires with a complex doctrine. It satisfies both our desire for nearness and our desire for otherness in God, while not diluting (as so many doctrines do) the power of either. Christianity doesn't melt the distinct aspects of God into a giant simple mass; it rather preserves them, in their full glory.

CHAPTER SEVEN
INDIVIDUALISM MEETS COLLECTIVISM: THE PSYCHOLOGY OF COMMUNITY

I've run into certain geniuses of individualism—they are very few and far between—who live their lives completely on their own terms; they are very powerful and have a great amount of happiness. We all should aspire to that.
Actor and Writer David Duchovny[1]

Our society has long been fond of the "self-made person." In fact, we practically worship the self-made person: the cultural hero who starts from nothing and makes her or his fortune by hard work and perseverance. Abraham Lincoln was a self-made person, a poor kid born in a log cabin who became president of the world's most powerful country through his hard work and ingenuity.

Recently, our love of the hypothetical rugged individualist has come somewhat under attack and for good reason: the self-made person is a myth. The rags-to-riches millionaire is not self-made; she is one of the lucky recipients of many gifts. She does not even plant the corn she eats; she does not make the wine she drinks; she does not cut the wood her house is built from. Further, she did not make her own intelligence nor the particular circumstances for which it was applied. A single accidental blow to the head or a nation-wide collapse of the industry for which she daringly risked everything, would un-make her world. Would someone then say she was self-unmade? No, she didn't make herself into what she is and she won't unmake herself. Like everyone, she will ride the winds of a world she did not create with a brain she did not create through a set of circumstances she did not create into a future she has minimal control over. In the words of Georgetown Professor and Author Michael Eric Dyson: "I don't believe in that kind of American John Wayne individualism where people pull themselves up by their bootstraps. Someone changed your diapers. And if that's the case, you ain't self-made."[2]

And yet to the casual observer of American culture, we frankly seem confused about what the heck we want. Although it might seem the tide is turning on American individualism, nonetheless the individualistic pathos is so deeply imbedded in our psyche that its effects are still seen everywhere. From childhood classroom traditions such as "show and tell" where students are encouraged to bring items that illustrate their uniqueness to American scientific norms such as "publish or perish" which put the focus on the individual's ability to succeed or fail, American society is pervaded by norms that reinforce the importance of the unique individual.[3] Thus, while few Americans want to end up (to borrow the quaint title from the famous book by Robert Putnam) *bowling alone,* it seems most Americans want to simultaneously (to borrow the words of David Duchovny) *live their life completely on their own terms and be powerful and happy.* It seems we could use some direction, a model to help us figure out what on earth we really *do* want—something to guide us through our strong desires for both individualism and collectivism.

Christianity provides a model that meets this complex duality. As we shall see, it meets both the desire for both human society *and* the desire for human individualism. It does so by keeping the truth in both views, while avoiding devastating consequences that follow if we hold one view to the exclusion of the other. It helps the human engine *run well.*

Atheists' Characterizations of Religion

Far from providing us meaningful goals, religions prescribe tribal values: amity for our tribe; enmity for other tribes; mind-closing faith; abject worship of authority.
Christopher Hitchens, *god is Not Great*[4]

Atheism...is the only sure way to regard all our fellow creatures as brothers and sisters.
Christopher Hitchens, *god is Not Great*[5]

Groups can have a powerful influence on us. If you don't believe that, try an experiment: Go to Chicago, find the nearest bar on Sunday, and watch a Packers/Bears football game. That'd be the *Chicago* Bears. Wait until the Packers score a touchdown, and then that's the cue for your little experiment—at that moment, in front of a large crowd of disappointed Bears fans drinking beer, you pull out your Packers' t-shirt, your giant Packers' foam finger; then go stand on the nearest chair and start yelling "WOOOOHOOOO!!! GOOOOO

PACKERS!!! Aaron Rodgers is the BEST!!!!" And be sure to wear one of those cheese hats. They love those.

No, please don't do that. I don't want you to experience excessive agony. But if you did do that, you'd discover first-hand the incredible power of group identity which so much research in my own field has explored. You'll discover that you will not be viewed as an individual in that moment by those Bears fans—they will not shout "we're all individuals here! Buy our individual friend here, who we view in only individual terms, a beer. Nice hat, you individual you!" No, you will not be treated as the specific person you are, but as a *Packer* fan. A part of a group.

And lest you think I'm picking on the good people of Chicago (for whom I have the highest regard), you'd find the same thing everywhere—try yelling "Hook 'em Horns" in College Station, Texas, or "Roll Tide" in Auburn, Alabama, or even "Go Griz" in Bozeman, Montana. Even here in the good ol' individualistic USA, collective identities matter—a lot. We cannot get away from them.

It is noteworthy that, while atheists rarely attack Christianity for being too individualistic, they have often attacked us for being too *collectivistic*. We are pictured as a kind of monolithic entity that encourages a tribal mentality—like hooligans beating up people from the opposite team at a soccer match. In this view, instead of producing a beautiful garden with all kinds of fruits and vegetables, we instead force the world to endure only *one* kind of vegetable. And it isn't even a good vegetable; it's something gross, like a radish. It's all radishes, radishes, radishes, dictated from the top down, forced on everyone. And all the beautiful strawberries are pulled up and killed, just for being strawberries.

The atheists are partially correct from a historical point of view. Christianity has a long and checkered history of force-feeding and bullying and killing in order to produce people who share a similar belief system. We would be dishonest fools to deny that, and I don't deny it.

However, this is not the whole story. The actual vision cast by Christianity—to which we have sometimes failed—isn't one that involves the top-down bludgeoning of people into a giant collectivistic mass. And in my own local experience in the Church, I have often seen glimpses of this larger beautiful vision, and Christianity has provided me a framework for understanding the psychological tensions I see in myself along these lines. When I have become too much of a lonely maverick (and that is my natural tendency), Christ has called me back into fellowship with others while reminding me that the hollow, propped-up conception of myself as a *maverick* is a myth (Luke 12:15; James 1:17). But when I have become too concerned with what others think—or thought that the collective comfort of believing the same thing as other people is somehow more important than the truth about who I am individually—Christ has reminded me that it is really what happens in private, when I am alone, that matters (Matthew 6:6).

From talking with other Christians and atheists, I know my experiences in the Church—which have been largely positive—are not the same as everyone else's. I know plenty of Christians who have been in churches where the mob mentality was ever-present. But it would be intellectually dishonest for me to pretend that has been my own experience. It hasn't been. In fact, I have often found more of a mob mentality, not in church, but in the academic circles I travel in. And it isn't just me. University of Virginia professor Jonathan Haidt (a well-respected and highly published academic) made quite a stir a few years ago when he argued, at the largest social psychology conference in the world, that social psychologists had a kind of liberal "tribal" mentality. The backlash for this was great—and ironic. People who do not have that mob mentality are the first to see it, and many social psychologists *do* see it. But the mob often doesn't consider itself a mob; it rather considers itself a group of reasonable people who have it all figured out.

Many social psychologists reacted to this obvious news of the potential for their own group bias with a rather alarming vitriol and an amusing lack of self-awareness. Personally, I have mostly been treated like a prince by my colleagues, so I do not want to present a false picture in your mind of my own experiences. The academia I live and breathe in is a wonderful place, but so is my church. However, I would feel more comfortable sharing a non-normative opinion at my church than I would sharing a non-normative opinion in academia. I worry about disagreeing with people in both places, but I worry about it a lot more in academic circles than in Christian circles.

Think for one second about the psychological implications of atheist Christopher Hitchens' quote: *Atheism is the only sure way to regard all our fellow creatures as brothers and sisters.* Why does he say that? Because the group psychology of religion is divisive? Fair enough—it can be. But Hitchens' solution would only work if everyone on earth became an atheist. Possibly, if everyone on earth became an atheist, the world would have less division. But it isn't because of anything unique in atheism—it's because we are more likely to regard people we agree with as brothers and sisters. It would be just as true for Hitchens to say *rhubarb worship is the only sure way to regard all our fellow creatures as brothers and sisters* or *loving the Chicago Bears is the only sure way to regard all our fellow creatures as brothers and sisters* or (gasp!) *Christianity is the only sure way to regard all our fellow creatures as brothers and sisters.* It doesn't matter what goes at the beginning of the sentence—if humanity all agreed on it, it would certainly aid our effort to consider everyone as brothers and sisters. That may include atheism, sure, but it also includes Christianity.

And for atheism to produce peace through that mechanism, it essentially requires the very uniformity of belief that Hitchens clearly does not like in religion. After all, reading his books, I'm not sure, as a deeply religious person, that I feel very good about the supposed non-divisive world he thinks he is creating—it is a world where, *just because I am religious*, I am—according to Hitchens[6]—to be viewed as *mind-closing* and *racist*, and what I believe is compared to (at best) *believing in the Abominable Snowman* and (at worst) to *child abuse*. Forgive me if I do not completely feel the spirit of universal brotherhood and sisterhood!

It doesn't matter what goes at the beginning of the sentence—if humanity all agreed on it, it would certainly aid our effort to consider everyone as brothers and sisters.

But I do not think that is all there is to it. Even if we all agreed on a primary belief system, the world would still have conflict. There would still be tensions between my freedom to do what I want with my yard and your desire for me not to put up a giant picture of Brett Favre that blocks your view of Soldier Field.

That's just a bit of backstory to the Christian vision. That backstory is important so you can see my own biases. I am aware of the long and difficult history Christians have had on this particular issue. Nonetheless, I believe the vision Christianity casts on this helps us understand and apply both sides of our psyche—and I'm going to tell you why.

Truly Optimal Distinctiveness: The Doctrine of the Body of Christ

People want to be unique. It would be hard to find anyone who would enthusiastically say, "I want to be exactly like everyone else in every possible way. I do not want to have any unique value. I wish every person had the same name and appearance so I would completely blend in."

But people also want to fit in. It would be equally difficult to find someone who would enthusiastically say, "I hope that, everywhere I go on earth, I am viewed as a thorn in the side of society; I want to be exactly the opposite of every single person, so I bear no resemblance at all to the rest of humanity. My inner longing is to be hated by everyone." And indeed, far from desiring to be hated, so deep is the human need to belong that research, even in individualistic countries, suggests people's self-esteem (or the degree to which they feel they have self-worth) is almost perfectly correlated to the degree to which they feel they "fit in" with some group.[7]

An interesting theory in psychology, called *Optimal Distinctiveness Theory*, suggests we reconcile these competing desires for uniqueness and belongingness by trying to find a balance between them.[8] The prototypical example of this process involves the wedding. During weddings, the average couple will keep most of the traditions of their existing culture—to belong, to fit in. Few people hold a wedding that disregards all traditional elements. Few people, for example, have their wedding in a poorly-lighted cave, wearing bright red sports jerseys or dressed as their favorite farm animals. Even the most radical diversions from the traditional cultural wedding often involve small concessions to tradition. Maybe the bride wears her mother's white dress and the groom avoids her that afternoon prior to the service.

However, most couples try to personalize the wedding, too. Even the most traditional, culture-bound weddings generally have some element that is unique to that couple. Maybe they choose a favorite but obscure Bible verse to have read, or get rid of the traditional cake in favor of a banana cream pie. Perhaps they have Uncle Tim play an old Journey song they like.

The wedding is thus a kind of parable to illustrate a larger point: People desire to fit in with others *and* to be unique at the same time. And *Optimal Distinctiveness Theory* says we are happiest when we find the best balance between those two desires, when we can keep part of the things that connect us to our culture and family but change just enough so we feel different, too. We want to fit in with tradition but also leave our personal mark on it.

Optimal Distinctiveness Theory is partially right; however, it doesn't go far enough. The optimal distinctiveness level that will make us happy is to maximize both belongingness and uniqueness, and sometimes this can be seen in compromise—a compromise that involves giving up part of your individuality and giving up part of fitting in. In that compromise, persons may still lose the parts of themselves they gave up, and may still likewise lose the part of fitting in that doesn't work for maintaining uniqueness. But what if no compromise is necessary? What if you can do both of those things at the same time? What if you can *completely* keep your distinctive individuality while, at the same time, *completely* retain the feeling of belonging?

The doctrine of the Body of Christ—that is, the Church—suggests this very thing is indeed possible. Paul gives a very detailed account of this idea in the 12th chapter of 1st Corinthians, which is worth repeating here in full:

> *The body is a unit, though it is made up of many parts; and though all its parts are many, they form one body. So it is with Christ. For we were all baptized by one Spirit into one body-whether Jews or Greeks, slave or free-and we were all given the one Spirit to drink. Now the body is not made up of one part but of many. If the foot should say, "Because I am not a hand, I do not belong to the body," it would not for that reason cease to be part of the body. And if the ear should say, "Because I am not an eye, I do not belong to the body," it would not for that reason cease to be part of the body. If the whole body were an eye, where would the sense of hearing be? If the whole body were an ear, where would the sense of smell be? But in fact God has arranged the parts in the body, every one of them, just as he wanted them to be. If they were all one part, where would the body be? As it is, there are many parts, but one body. The eye cannot say to the hand, "I don't need you!" And the head cannot say to the feet, "I don't need you!" On the contrary, those parts of the body that seem to be weaker are indispensable, and the parts that we think are less honorable we treat with special honor. And the parts that are unpresentable are treated with special modesty, while our presentable parts need no special treatment. But God has combined the members of the body and has given greater honor to the parts that lacked it, so that there should be no division in the body,*

but that its parts should have equal concern for each other. If one part suffers, every part suffers with it; if one part is honored, every part rejoices with it.

In other words: We are all wildly *different*, and yet we are not *independent.* It is hard to imagine two things as different in form and function as the eye and the elbow, and yet they are connected to the same body. You can be gloriously different from everyone and yet completely needed by everyone. You can be simultaneously completely individualistic and collectivistic. You feel the need for uniqueness. You are completely unique, irreplaceable. You feel the need for belonging. You do belong somewhere; completely, totally, fully belong.

We are all wildly *different*, and yet we are not *independent.*

Two Disasters Avoided by the Body of Christ

Sometimes the value of an idea can be highlighted by pointing out what happens when it is ignored. It is possible that doctrines can encourage individualism without considering connectedness. It is also possible that they can encourage connectedness without considering the value of the individual. What happens in these cases?

Individualism-Run-Wild versus the Body

Religion is the best antidote to the individualism of the consumer age. The idea that society can do without it flies in the face of history and, now, evolutionary biology.

Professor and Rabbi Jonathan Sacks[9]

Let's first consider the individualistic perspective that is endemic in our own American culture, expressed in the myth of the self-made person and, also, expressed well by John Stuart Mill in the first chapter of his book, *On Liberty*:

"The only part of the conduct of anyone for which he is amenable to society is that which concerns others. In the part which merely concerns himself,

his independence is, of right, absolute. Over himself, over his own body and mind, the individual is sovereign."

Is he? C.S. Lewis pictured humans like a fleet of ships sailing to a destination.[10] In our modern society, we have focused much of our attention on the individual ships. But we often forget we aren't sailing alone. This isn't just a matter of mere personal choice: Other people are there whether we like them to be or not. And if we don't take them into consideration, we will be rudely introduced at close range, and that unpleasant crash will mean the ruin of our own ship. It is not possible thus to sail our little boat in an exclusively individualistic manner. This individualism-run-wild, this turning a blind eye to the way the whole fits together, can lead to nothing but shipwrecks. Even Mill recognized that we must consider the other ships.

These shipwrecks can be seen on multiple levels. For example, most people engage in what psychologists call *self-enhancement*: They view themselves as better than objective evidence would suggest they *ought to* view themselves. So, let's say objective evidence suggests I am an average Boggle player; however, I'm prone to think I'm above average.

Certain people are particularly prone to a kind of hyper-individualism that makes them think they are better than they are. If you think about it, our society is trying to produce that kind of person: The rugged individualist who "believes in himself" and disregards other people's opinions is often hailed as an ideal. Watch American TV commercials for 10 minutes, and you will repeatedly hear how great you are, that you deserve it, and it's all about you. This disconnected self-enhancer is exactly the kind of thing we are trying to produce.

And yet, research shows the following thing: When we meet that person in reality, we hate them.[11] We think they are pompous jerks. They are a ship without a rudder, and they run into everyone in exactly the wrong way. It is a sad irony that our culture is trying to create a person not one of us likes when we meet him face to face.

It is a sad irony that our culture is trying to create a person not one of us likes when we meet him face to face.

Or take the narcissist who loves himself above all else. Common cultural wisdom says we must love ourselves first. But what happens when someone truly loves themselves above all? What happens when that kind of disconnected individualism-run-wild is exhibited by the narcissist?

Research suggests, among other things, narcissistic people are likely to end up in jail as violent criminals.[12] They are an individualistic ship without a rudder, but society is comprised of other ships, and they eventually will hurt them—and face repercussions themselves.

The Doctrine of the Body of Christ keeps the ships both individually content *and* in harmony with each other. By meeting the deeper need for uniqueness and the need for connectedness, Christian doctrine avoids the pratfalls of individualism-run-wild. We are unique, but we also must consider the larger body we are a part of.

The Borg versus the Body

It should be said that the truth which remains when things are destroyed is the truth of the divine intellect, and this is absolutely one in number. The truth which is in things or in the soul, however, varies according to the variety of things.
St. Thomas Aquinas[13]

In resisting this horrible theory of the Soul of the Hive, we of Christendom stand not for ourselves, but for all of humanity; for the essential and distinctive human idea that one good and happy man is an end in himself, that a soul is worth saving.
G. K. Chesterton[14]

Consider a more collectivistic point of view that suggests, as Aristotle did, "neither must we suppose that any one of the citizens belongs to himself, for all belong to the state, and are each of them a part of the state, and the care of each part is inseparable from the care of the whole."[15] In the futuristic world of *Star Trek* there is an entity called the Borg. Although made up of millions of individual persons, the Borg functions through a hive mind—all voices coalescing into one. Borg are driven entirely by one goal: the collective goal. The Borg exists only for the Borg. Individuals are irrelevant as individuals, for they exist only for the collective.

Though no human society goes to such an extreme, some groups are closer to the collective mentality than others. And I'd like you to see the end result of that idea: *It will not work.* This attention to the collective fleet at the expense of the individual ships is ultimately disastrous, for if the individual ships decay and rot, eventually the whole fleet will fail. If one ship loses a rudder, it will crash into the others. So just as we cannot consider only the individual ships, we also cannot only consider the fleet as a whole.

Christianity's idea of the Body is nothing like the Borg. I must be careful here. There are cultural elements people mean when they say "collectivism" that I am not addressing. For example, by collectivism often researchers (including myself) have meant behavioral practices such as whether people tend to live with their grandparents.[16] Christianity has little to say about these sorts of practices, and I do not think as Christians we should be practicing a kind of cultural imperialism whereby we make our own somewhat random and irrelevant practices into "Christian" ones.

I am not attacking particular practices but the worldview that does not account for individual uniqueness. And, in as much as the collectivistic view says the group matters more than the individual, the collectivistic view is wrong. The Cross stands as a universal testimony that I—I as an individual—matter. Christ loved the world collectively, yes, but he also loved *me personally*. His death and resurrection apply to me individually. Jesus said: "Are not five sparrows sold for a penny? Yet not one of them is forgotten by God. Indeed, the very hairs of your head are all numbered. Don't be afraid; you are worth more than many sparrows" (Luke 12:6-7). You see, I, Lucian Conway, am not forgotten by God. There is no other me on the earth. If my voice does not sing in harmony with God's, no other can ever replace it. God knows the hairs on my head, and I can be certain not a single sparrow dies outside of God's presence.

We are Different and Yet the Same

Because every man is a biped, fifty men are not a centipede.[17]
G. K. Chesterton

The same should be said about colors, because they too are properly called visible, although they are only seen because of one light.
St. Thomas Aquinas[18]

There is another sense, too, in which Christianity maintains the best elements of Individualism and Collectivism. Christianity does not argue that people are completely different in every way. Indeed, that would be colossally stupid: Our similarities are obvious. Being *human* means sharing certain features that distinguish us from other creatures in this universe.

The real question for our purposes here, though, isn't "what features do we share" but rather "what features *ought* we share?" What does Christianity teach about how human society would be, if all were perfect?

Christianity clearly affirms the fact that every parent of multiple children will tell you: For reasons we cannot fully explain, people are different from each other. The real question is: So how are we, a collection of uniquely different individuals, to function together? Some people may imagine Christianity teaches that, as we follow Christ, we all become much more like each other, so we essentially lose our unique personalities. That is untrue. If you are destined to be a perfect eye, the more you become perfect, the more eye-like you will be. Importantly, the more you will be clearly different from an elbow. Following Christ heightens individual differences. To borrow from G. K. Chesterton's metaphor, it is only in the sin-stained morass that the elbow and the eye both decompose into the same material, and become indistinguishable. In the living Body of Christ, they remain forever unique.

As we become more like Christ, there is also a sense in which we will become more like each other—a moral sense. That is, as Christ changes us, we all become more loving, more kind, more merciful, as He is. We experience the deepest and best part of the universal human reservoir. However, the Christian answer—unlike many religious answers—does not make us lose our individuality in the process. In fact, it celebrates it, it honors it, it suggests that it is necessary for the healthy functioning of the Church.

Thus, Christianity clearly brings out both our common humanity and our individual uniqueness. It is not intended to pretend we will become completely different from everyone in every way, for if that were true, there would be no common features we could call "human." Christianity simultaneously makes me a perfect *human* and a perfect *me.* It grows those features which God intended all humans to share, but it also grows those features I alone was meant to hold.

In summary, Christian doctrine helps bring together the glory of collectivism and the beauty of individualism. It teaches we were in fact made to fully belong to a community; but we were also made to be utterly and uniquely irreplaceable. As such, by accounting for both sides of human psychology, it helps the human machine run well.

CHAPTER EIGHT
THE LANDSCAPE AND THE MAP

On our honeymoon to Switzerland, one of the places my wife Kathrene and I really wanted to see was called Blue Lake. We were staying in Kandersteg, and my wife said she had seen a brochure that Blue Lake was a 45-minute leisurely walk.

So we set off on our *45 minute leisurely walk*. Only it turned out not to be 45 minutes. And it was in no conceivable way leisurely. No, our pleasant stroll ended up being a *10-hour* grueling hike through the Swiss Alps. To make matters worse, it rained on us. On slippery high mountain slopes, we nearly fell to our deaths a couple of times—literally. I was already imagining the headlines in my hometown paper: *Stupid Couple Dies in Wilderness.* (Subtitle: *We Knew That Dumb Guy Would Be the Death of That Beautiful Woman*). And then, by the time we got to Blue Lake, it was too dark to see it.

In summary: *This was not a good day.*

After setting out on what was supposed to be a leisurely morning stroll, we arrived back at our hotel in Kandersteg in the middle of the following night. We were exhausted. We were wet. We were cold. We were hungry. We were more than a little frazzled because we were too late to catch the last bus and were thus forced to hitchhike back with some very nice French guys whom, for a brief second, we thought might kidnap us. (It turned out that they were so nice that they refused to accept our repeated attempts to pay them for their trouble. French guys, if you are reading this—thank you. Sorry we thought you might be psychopathic kidnappers.)

Now here is a test to see if you understand relationships. There we were, wet, hungry, exhausted, walking in the door of our hotel at 3:00 in the morning. What do you think the first thing that happened was?

If you said *you got a bite to eat and went to bed*, you've obviously never been in a serious relationship. Because I'll tell you what happened. The moment we walked in the door of our room, I turned to Kathrene and said these words:

"Find that brochure! You know, the one that said it was a '45-minute leisurely walk'? We're not doing ANYTHING until I see that brochure RIGHT NOW."

My wife is an easy-going and thoughtful woman with a very good temperament, and so—much to her everlasting credit—she (without complaint) dug around in her stuff in our room and found the brochure. And, sure enough, it *did* say it was a 45-minute leisurely walk to Blue Lake. But there was a problem.

She had picked up the brochure in Kander*grund*.

And we were staying in Kander*steg*.

So, you see, if you get on a train from where we were staying in Kandersteg and get off in Kandergrund, it really is by all accounts a nice walk through the woods to Blue Lake. But if you start *walking* from Kandersteg, there is a pretty big mountain in the way. Gear up for an adventure.

Now if Kathrene and I had taken the time to look at a map—to get the big picture overview—we would have never made that mistake. It's incredibly easy to get confused by words on a brochure if you don't have the larger picture in your head. If we had bothered to learn anything about local topography, we would have thought something suspicious was happening when we started our walk from Kandersteg.

As humans, we can easily get too focused on the part that says "45 minutes" that we forget to look at the map of the Alps. In this book, I aimed to provide a wide, high altitude overview of the psychological landscape. I've intentionally shied away from specific words on the brochure and focused instead on the lay of the land. I want you to reflect on the bigger picture of what Christianity says, *writ large*, about what makes the human machine run well. The question I've tried to answer was: Given the landscape of the human mind and the map of Christian thought and belief, do those landscapes match? Is Christianity a good map for navigating the complex landscape that is… *us*?

Atheists and Christians in the Larger Landscape

As it happens, atheists sometimes grow frustrated with any religious reference to the big picture. Critics of Christianity often see this kind of big picture talk as an attempt to ignore the tough bits and focus only on those parts of our religion we want to see. Atheist Dan Barker rather mockingly said the following about the Christian response to difficult Biblical passages (from *God: The Most Unpleasant Character in All Fiction*):

> *They think "The Bible" is an intact and coherent book, a unitary "Word of God" that explains itself harmoniously no matter which author you are reading. A verse or two might seem shockingly immoral up close but, stepping back, we can see God's grander plan and know that although he is uncompromising in his holiness, he is actually a wise, merciful, forgiving Father.*[1]

Their frustration is reasonable to some degree. Part of what atheists are responding to is a piecemeal approach that does not do a very good job of considering the big picture. Barker goes on to give an example:

> *When I ask those believers to give me the context of a troublesome passage, they often produce a verse from another part of the Bible—sometimes written centuries later in another language and country, with a different agenda—such as "Whoever does not love does not know God, for God is love."*[2]

In other words, what frustrates Barker isn't that there is an attempt at a coherent account—it's the *lack* of one. It's a hand wave at a particular problem by making reference to an instance or two that seems to counteract it. And the critics are partially right; all too often, we do *exactly* that.

Don't get me wrong. I understand the temptation to take atheists like Barker on point-by-point in a somewhat piecemeal fashion. For example, in his book *God: The Most Unpleasant Character in All Fiction*,[3] Barker is clearly upset by (a) God's jealousy and (b) the conditional nature of God's love for us. It may perhaps come as a shock to him that neither of those things bothers me in the slightest. (a) If I was an unfaithful husband, I would *want* my wife to be jealous—a lack of jealousy would not mean she loved me more—it would mean she loved me less. Jealousy seems to me the natural response to the breaking of a healthy love relationship. Its complete absence would not be love—but *apathy*. (b) I'm not troubled in the least by the fact that the Bible says repeatedly that I cannot experience God's love if I choose to walk away from it. My experience of love in that sense *must* be conditional. It doesn't seem inconsistent to me at all to say (as the Bible does) that God cannot stop loving me and to also say (as the Bible does) I will not *experience* that love if I actively reject it.

And many of the so-called "negative attributes" of God strike me like that. But if I try to attack those things piecemeal, I'd be falling into a game of *What Point Do You Emphasize?* which I said in Chapter One I was trying to avoid. And I'd also miss the larger point that atheists make, a point that is worth considering and that I take very seriously—sometimes God's behavior doesn't seem palatable to us. Some of the verses Barker mentions *do* bother me. So, I'd like to end this book by focusing on the big picture landscape and not on a few of the debatable brochures.

Is Painting a Larger Landscape a Viable Goal?

It is clear in many atheist attacks that they do not merely think we fail to capture the big picture—they actually think a big picture landscape of the Bible is not possible. They aren't just challenging some specific verse—they claim Christianity is hopelessly contradictory. Are they right? Is it a viable goal to focus on the big picture of religion, or is it just a big mess? You would literally have to have been asleep as you read this book if you did not already know I think it *is* reasonable to paint the religious landscape with a large brush. There is no definitive standard for coherence, but I ask you to think about the standard for yourself for a moment by way of an example the atheists themselves often use.

No one—not even a committed anti-religious atheist like Barker—denies that the Bible repeatedly says God loves us. It says it from the beginning of the book to the end. Christians have, for centuries, maintained that God's love is perfect, unending, and pure—and the Bible backs that claim up. It isn't a "minor" theme.

Atheists attack this notion frequently by pointing out specific difficult verses. They wonder how many uncomfortable verses it takes for us to give up on God? How many times must God appear unloving in the Bible before we give up on Him entirely? Fair enough. I actually do consider those difficult verses in the landscape of our view of God and have tried to discuss that in the pages of this book.

But it is an honest question to ask in return: How many verses about God's *love* does it take for an atheist to admit that any discussion of the landscape of the Bible *must* include that fact? What is the standard in reverse for admission of *coherence* or consistency? It is the larger landscape that truly matters. What qualifies as a landscape, if a constant theme reflected from beginning to end does not? If the topography in Switzerland includes a lot of mountains, is it reasonable to conclude there is no consistent topography because it also includes some plains? Are we forced to ignore the obvious consistent mountain "feel" of Switzerland because there is *more* to Swiss landscapes than *just* mountains? At what point does it become rather silly to ignore the mountains out of my window at nearly every train stop? Consider for a moment this statement by Barker (from *God: The Most Unpleasant Character in All Fiction*):

At what point does it become rather silly to ignore the mountains out of my window at nearly every train stop?

> *It is not hard to find contrasting verses, but how can a handful of sycophantic praises mitigate hundreds of cruel commands and bloodcurdling barbarities? Actions speak louder than words. If Yahweh behaves like a thug, his reputation can't be redeemed by one of his minions simply parroting "God is love."*[4]

Now I quite agree with Barker about the importance of actions. One of my own personal mantras is *words are cheap.* But I am left to wonder what mountain range would loom large enough to count in Barker's landscape as a coherent narrative—if the standard for judging God's behavior is truly *action.* I have read the book in question, too, from cover to cover—and when I finished reading the book *in its entirety*, I found that God is depicted as literally taking on human form and *dying for me.* Now, the nature of that death is controversial and complicated, but there is no denying that it has always been depicted by Christians—and by the Bible—as God *suffering* for us. God took *action* to show His love for us at great cost to Himself. His suffering in our place is one of the most consistent themes of the New Testament.

My point is this: I do not deny that sometimes God appears to me as "thuggish" in the Bible in ways I don't understand. I consider that as part of the equation. But it seems to me that Barker denies the vast mountain range within the landscape, too—the vast landscape of God's love and mercy. Atheists often act like those verses simply don't matter somehow, but they are not only as beautiful as the Swiss Alps—they are also as vast and numerous. And in this book, in each chapter I have tried to paint large landscapes that help us see the bigger contours of Christian teaching—and I think that enterprise is legitimate.

The Conclusion of the Matter: Where I Oddly Tell You to Stop Listening to Me

Very well then, atheism is too simple.
C. S. Lewis[5]

Once, when I was on a job interview, an anti-religious professor (obviously unaware I was a Christian) mocked his Christian students by saying: "They are so simple-minded: They believe that killing in one circumstance might be morally ok, yet in another circumstance it would be morally wrong. Simple-minded idiots! If only they could have my more complex view that killing is always wrong all the time."

I didn't have the heart to tell him the obvious truth: His students may or may not be wrong, but they were *certainly* more complex than he was. To believe in a nuanced application of the murder principle is more complex than to believe in a simple-minded rule. His simple belief that killing was morally wrong 100% of the time ignores instances of killing in self-defense or in the defense of innocent life. It also turns a blind eye to the fact that there are those who would gladly destroy life, if given the chance, which means we live in a world where killing an evil person is, sadly, sometimes necessary to preserve the lives of others.

I often feel rather like that when hearing atheists talk about what I believe. They throw around words about how simple we are—using the simplest language possible. They attack us for being too narrow—

and pitch a much narrower vision. They ignore the nuances of human psychology, which our religion exists to help people navigate—and seem to believe that if they *wish* humans were different, they *are* different.

All of that occasionally leaves me feeling a bit like C. S. Lewis when he said "atheism is too simple." I know atheists themselves are not simple-minded people, but their attacks on Christianity often ignore the complexities of human psychology. In this book, I have attempted to open a discussion about big-picture landscape issues where I think Christianity helps human beings run well. In so doing, I have tried to focus on the things that loom large in both human psychology and in Christian thinking. I am not in denial about what the Bible says about God—quite the contrary. I want to show both sides of Christian teaching because I think both sides match dilemmas in human psychology. I am not closing my eyes to the fact that God is sometimes depicted as angry and difficult. I do not think anger necessarily unloving, just as I do not think justice is necessarily lacking in compassion. I do not think individualism is necessarily non-collective, and I do not think prayer necessarily excludes the plow. I do not think open-mindedness necessarily excludes closed-mindedness or vice versa. I do not think reliance on authority excludes empirical observation. And I do not think common sense boundaries exclude passionate joy.

I have found quite a measure of deep and lasting peace in following Jesus's teaching. He has instilled in me a wondrous complex simplicity, and it is only in truly following Him that my own machine has run well. A lot of other people would say the same. And while this is not definitive evidence that Christianity is true, it is at least evidence enough to give thinking people pause about atheists' claim that religion breaks the human machine. Far from breaking it, Christian teachings help balance the discrepant mess that is the human psyche and set it on solid ground.

But don't listen to me—or the atheists—or anybody. Before dismissing the claims made in this book, I urge you to test them in your own life. Reflect deeply, think hard, and then see if I'm right. Frankly, maybe it is time you stopped listening to *all* of us and found out for yourself. I believe if you do that and seek God, you too will find beauty in Christ's complex simplicity.

DISCUSSION QUESTIONS

Chapter 1

1. Whether you are a Christian or an Atheist or somewhere in between, have you ever had discussions with people about religion? When people dispute religion, do they tend to use arguments about practical psychology or arguments about philosophy and reason?

2. Do you think the effectiveness of something is a compelling argument for its truth?

3. Do you feel comfortable saying "I don't know" when asked questions? At what points in your own life have you (if ever) dismissed other people's opinions because they said they didn't know the answer to a basic question?

4. The author states that Christianity integrates *good* parts of the human psyche. What do you think it would do with purely *bad* parts of the human psyche? Would its view be more complex or less complex than, say, the typical atheists' view?

Chapter 2

1. In what ways do you think, in your own life, being closed-minded has been helpful? In what ways has it been harmful?

2. Do you think your experience with the Church suggests the Biblical model of combining open- and closed-mindedness?

3. About what sort of beliefs do you think it is important to be particularly closed-minded? Do other people you know feel the same about those beliefs?

Chapter 4

1. Do you think it is fair to characterize atheists' belief in facts as "religious" in their nature? Why or why not?

2. Given that common sense can sometimes go wrong, how do you determine when it is right or wrong?

3. Do you think revelations from God are based in authority, common sense, empirical observation, all of those things, or something else entirely?

4. Discuss your own feelings about where you believe your own knowledge comes from. Is there one "source" you have learned to trust more than others, and if so, do you think you would benefit from considering the more complex view discussed in this chapter?

Chapter 4

1. What are the boundaries in your life that have produced a sense of psychological freedom?

2. Consider what freedom means. After communism fell in Russia, the system was more free in the political sense, but people had a harder time getting food. Was that freedom?

3. Do you think Christianity uniquely helps balance boundaries and freedom, or could that balance be found just as easily without it?

4. The author has talked a lot about practical balance that might apply across multiple kinds of belief systems. But is God necessary in your experience for joy?

5. What are the *cookie doughs* of your life – those things that you truly love and that give you real positive joy? Do you ever feel the tensions discussed in this chapter?

Chapter 5

1. The author repeatedly uses *fairyland* as a metaphor to describe the Christian view of the spiritual realm. Do you think this metaphor is appropriate? What ways would you describe the unseen world?

2. Not everyone sees life as a fairytale. Do you think this is a useful way to picture your life, or the life of other people? For people who don't care about fairytales, does this approach matter at all?

3. Do you think the author is fair to the atheist alternative vision? Do you find it compelling as a way to find meaning without spirit? Do you think the Christian vision is truly more expansive?

Chapter 6

1. Do you ever feel God's absence and if so, how do you deal with it?

2. Do you feel more frustrated by depictions of God's anger or by depictions of God's inaction?

3. Some of the Bible verses describing God's anger, especially in the Old Testament, can be graphic and disturbing. Do you think the author is fair in his method of dealing with those verses?

Chapter 7

1. Talk about ways you feel the need to be an individual and the need to be a part of a group. How have *you* balanced those things?

2. Are there other passages in the Bible that might provide a different model of individualism and collectivism than the one the author discusses?

3. Do you think the author's depiction of American society as hyper-individualistic is fair? How would you characterize this issue?

Chapter 8

1. Do you think the big picture critique of atheists is fair? Do you think the Bible is simply too incoherent to create a larger narrative?

2. Can you think of any other ways the Bible might help balance psychological tensions, besides the ones discussed in this book? What other parts of human psychology that the author does *not* discuss might be aided by a Christian outlook?

About Lucian Gideon Conway, III

Dr. Lucian Gideon Conway III received his Ph.D. in Social Psychology from the University of British Columbia in 2001. He is an internationally-known psychology researcher who specializes in work on cognitive complexity and culture. His scientific work on the complexity of political figures has been featured in popular media outlets such as the *Washington Post, USA Today, and BBC Radio*. Further, Dr. Conway's scientific work has appeared in some of the most influential psychology journals in the world, including *American Psychologist*, *Journal of Personality and Social Psychology*, *Personality and Social Psychology Bulletin*, *Personality and Social Psychology Review*, and *Journal of Experimental Social Psychology*. He has been interviewed on *National Public Radio* and has given invited talks at the University of Michigan-Ann Arbor, Purdue University, and the Wilderness Society. In addition, Dr. Conway was chosen by the *Department of Homeland Security* to head a prestigious team of the top researchers in the world to study the linguistic patterns of radical group leaders. He is currently a tenured Full Professor of Psychology at the University of Montana.

More information on Dr. Conway's scientific work, links to news articles and academic papers, and his CV, can be found here: http://psychweb.psy.umt.edu/conway/

References

Chapter 1

[1] Cited in: Konner, J. (2007). *The Atheist's Bible: An Illustrious Collection of Irreverent Thoughts.* New York: Harper Collins.

[2] Russell, B. (1967). *Why I am Not A Christian.* New Yorkp: Simon and Schuster.

[3] Ask Atheists (2016). *Top quotes.* Retrieved from http://www.askatheists.com/atheist-quotes

[4] Russell, B. (1967). *Why I am Not A Christian.* New York: Simon and Schuster.

[5] Hitchens, C. (2007). *god is Not Great: How Religion Poisons Everything.* New York: Twelve Books.

[6] Dawkins, R. (2008). *The God Delusion.* New York: First Mariner Books.

[7] Shermer, M. (2015). *The Moral Arc: How Science Makes Us Better People.* New York: Henry Holt and Company.

[8] Stenger, V. J. (2012). *God and the Folly of Faith: The Incompatibility of Science and Religion.* Amherst, NY: Prometheus Books.

[9] Barker, Dan (2016). *God: The Most Unpleasant Character in All Fiction.* New York: Sterling Press.

[10] Dennett, D. C. (2007). *Breaking the Spell: Religion as a Natural Phenomenon.* New York: Penguin Books.

[11] Hitchens, C. (2007). *god is Not Great: How Religion Poisons Everything.* New York: Twelve Books.

[12] Russell, B. (1967). *Why I am Not A Christian.* New York: Simon and Schuster.

[13] Harris, S. (2011). *The Moral Landscape: How Science Can Determine Human Values.* New York: Free Press.

[14] Conway, L. G., III. (2011). Grading common arguments for God's existence. *Apologetic Professor*. Retrieved from http://www.apologeticprofessor.com/articles/2011/11/grading-common-arguments-for-god%e2%80%99s-existence-part-i/

[15] Peng, K. & Nisbett, R. (1999). Culture, dialectics, and reasoning about contradiction. *American Psychologist*, 54, 741-754.

[16] All Bible references throughout this book are to the *New International Version.*

[17] Dennett, D. C. (2007). *Breaking the Spell: Religion as a Natural Phenomenon.* New York: Penguin Books.

[18] Chesterton, G. K. (1909). *Orthodoxy*. London: John Lane Company.

[19] Cited in: Konner, J. (2007). *The Atheist's Bible: An Illustrious Collection of Irreverent Thoughts*. New York: Harper Collins.

[20] Conway, L. G., III. (2014). The Apologetic Professor's argument for atheism. *Apologetic Professor*. Retrieved from: http://www.apologeticprofessor.com/articles/2014/09/the-apologetic-professors-argument-for-atheism/

[21] Conway, L. G., III. (2014). From the reader mailbag: Why I believe in Jesus and not Osiris. *Apologetic Professor*. Retrieved from http://www.apologeticprofessor.com/articles/2013/01/from-the-reader-mailbag-why-i-believe-in-jesus-and-not-osiris/

[22] Dawkins, R. (2008). *The God Delusion.* New York: First Mariner Books.

[23] Chesterton, G. K. (1909). *Orthodoxy*. London: John Lane Company.

[24] Chadwick, H. (translator). (1991). *The Confessions of St. Augustine.* New York: Oxford University Press.

[25] Cited in: WorldNetDaily (2005). Bill Maher: Christians have neurological disorder. *WorldNetDaily*. Retrieved from: http://www.wnd.com/2005/02/28970/

[26] Conway, L. G., III, Houck, S. C., Gornick, L. J., & Repke, M. A. (2016). Ideologically-motivated perceptions of complexity: Believing those who agree with you are more complex than they are. *Journal of Language and Social Psychology, 35*, 708-718.

[27] Suedfeld, P., Tetlock, P. E., & Streufert, S. (1992). Conceptual/integrative complexity. In C. P. Smith (Ed.) *Motivation and personality: Handbook of thematic content analysis*. Cambridge: Cambridge University Press.

[28] For a summary of the validation of the integrative complexity construct, see: Conway, L. G., III, Conway, K. R., Gornick, L. J., & Houck, S. C. (2014). Automated integrative complexity. *Political Psychology, 35*, 603-624. See also Houck, S. C., Conway, L. G., III, & Gornick, L. J. (2014). Automated integrative complexity: Current challenges and future directions. *Political Psychology, 35*, 647-659.

[29] Suedfeld, P., & Tetlock, P. (1977). Integrative complexity of communications in international crises. *Journal of Conflict Resolution, 21*, 169-184.

[30] For a summary, see: Conway, L. G., III, Suedfeld, P., & Tetlock, P. E. (2001). Integrative complexity and political decisions that lead to war or peace. In D. J. Christie, R. V. Wagner, & D. Winter (Eds.), *Peace, conflict, and violence: Peace psychology for the 21st century* (pp. 66-75). Englewood Cliffs, NJ: Prentice-Hall.

[31] For example, see: Conway, L. G., III, Gornick, L. J., Houck, S. C., Hands Towgood, K., & Conway, K. R. (2011). The hidden implications of radical group rhetoric: Integrative complexity and terrorism. *Dynamics of Asymmetric Conflict, 4*, 155-165. [Reprinted in Smith, A. (Ed.), *The Relationship Between Rhetoric and Terrorist Violence*. New York: Routledge.]

[32] Davidson, K., Livingstone, S., McArthur, K., Dickson, L., & Gumley, A. (2007). An integrative complexity analysis of cognitive behaviour therapy sessions for borderline personality disorder. *Psychology and Psychotherapy, 80*, 513-523.

[33] Conway, L. G., III, Gornick, L. J., Burfiend, C., Mandella, P., Kuenzli, A., Houck, S. C., & Fullerton, D. T. (2012). Does simple rhetoric win elections? An integrative complexity analysis of U.S. presidential campaigns. *Political Psychology, 33*, 599-618.

[34] Repke, M. A., Conway, L. G., III, & Houck, S. C. (2017). The strategic manipulation of linguistic complexity: A test of two models of lying. *Journal of Language and Social Psychology. Advance online publication. DOI: 10.1177/0261927X17706943*

[35] Conway, L. G., III, & Liht, J. (2005, July). Does religious conversion make people less complex? In L.G. Conway, III, & Jose Liht (Chairs),

Fundamentalism and beyond: The relationship between religion and politics. Symposium conducted at the 28th Annual Meeting of the International Society of Political Psychology, Toronto, Canada.

[36] Conway, L. G., III. (2007, July). *The causes of complex thinking: Integrative complexity, politics, and religion.* Symposium conducted at the 30th Annual Meeting of the International Society of Political Psychology, Portland, USA.

[37] Houck, S.C., Conway, L.G. III, Repke, M.A., Parrow, K., Allison, A., & Lorentzen, E. (in preparation). *The complexity of famous religious and irreligious persons: Comparing perception and reality.*

[38] Conway, L. G., III, & Thoemmes, F. (2005, July). Integrative complexity of three extremely religious U.S. Presidents. In L.G. Conway, III, & Jose Liht (Chairs), *Fundamentalism and beyond: The relationship between religion and politics.* Symposium conducted at the 28th Annual Meeting of the International Society of Political Psychology, Toronto, Canada.

[39] Houck, S.C., Conway, L.G. III, Repke, M.A., Parrow, K., Allison, A., & Lorentzen, E. (in preparation). *The complexity of famous religious and irreligious persons: Comparing perception and reality.*

[40] Conway, L. G., III, & Thoemmes, F. (2005, July). Integrative complexity of three extremely religious U.S. Presidents. In L.G. Conway, III, & Jose Liht (Chairs), *Fundamentalism and beyond: The relationship between religion and politics.* Symposium conducted at the 28th Annual Meeting of the International Society of Political Psychology, Toronto, Canada.

[41] Pancer, S. M., Jackson, L. M., Hunsberger, B., Pratt, M. W., et al. (1995). Religious orthodoxy and the complexity of thought about religious and nonreligious issues. *Journal of Personality, 63*, 213-232.

[42] Liht, J., Conway, L. G. III, Savage, S., White, W., O'Neill, K. A. (2011). Religious fundamentalism: An empirically derived construct and measurement scale. *Archive for the Psychology of Religion, 33*, 299-323.

[43] For example, see: Gruenfeld, D.H. (1995). Status, Ideology, and Integrative Complexity on the U.S. Supreme Court: Rethinking the Politics of Political Decision Making. *Journal of Personality and Social Psychology, 68*, 5-20.

[44] For example, see: Conway, L. G., III., Thoemmes, F., Allison, A. M., Hands Towgood, K., Wagner, M. J., Davey, K., Salcido, A., Stovall, A. N., Dodds, D. P., Bongard, K, & Conway, K. R. (2008). Two ways to be

complex and why they matter: Implications for attitude strength and lying. *Journal of Personality and Social Psychology, 95,* 1029-1044.

[45] For example, see: Conway, L. G., III, Schaller, M., Tweed, R. G., & Hallett, D. (2001). The complexity of thinking across cultures: Interactions between culture and situational context. *Social Cognition, 19*, 230-253. See also Conway, L. G., Gornick, L. J., Houck, S. C., Anderson, C., Stockert, J., Sessoms, D. and McCue, K. (2015). Are conservatives really more simple-minded than liberals? The domain specificity of complex thinking. *Political Psychology.* doi: 10.1111/pops.12304

[46] Conway, L. G., III, Houck, S. C., Gornick, L. J., & Repke, M. A. (2016). Ideologically-motivated perceptions of complexity: Believing those who agree with you are more complex than they are. *Journal of Language and Social Psychology, 35,* 708-718.

Chapter 2

[1] Cited in: Konner, J. (2007). *The Atheist's Bible: An Illustrious Collection of Irreverent Thoughts.* New York: Harper Collins.

[2] Cited in: Konner, J. (2007). *The Atheist's Bible: An Illustrious Collection of Irreverent Thoughts.* New York: Harper Collins.

[3] Cited in: Konner, J. (2007). *The Atheist's Bible: An Illustrious Collection of Irreverent Thoughts.* New York: Harper Collins.

[4] Barker, Dan (2016). *God: The Most Unpleasant Character in All Fiction.* New York: Sterling Press.

[5] Dennett, D. C. (2007). *Breaking the Spell: Religion as a Natural Phenomenon.* New York: Penguin Books.

[6] Bugliosi, V. (2011). *Divinity of Doubt: The God Question.* New York: Vanguard Press.

[7] Cited in: Oden, T. C., & Crosby, C. (2007). *Ancient Christian Devotional: A Year of Weekly Readings.* Downer's Grove, Illinois: Intervarsity Press.

[8] Cited in: Oden, T. C., & Crosby, C. (2007). *Ancient Christian Devotional: A Year of Weekly Readings.* Downer's Grove, Illinois: Intervarsity Press.

[9] Tetlock, P.E., Armor, D., & Peterson, R. S. (1995). The slavery debate in antebellum America: Cognitive style and the limits of compromise. *Journal of Personality and Social Psychology, 66*, 115-126. Also see: Tetlock, P. E. (1986). A value pluralism model of ideological reasoning, *Journal of Personality and Social Psychology, 50*, 819-827.

[10] Tetlock, P. E., & Tyler, A. (1996). Churchill's cognitive and rhetorical style: The debates over Nazi intentions and self-government for India. *Political Psychology, 17*, 149-170.

[11] Tetlock, P. E., & Tyler, A. (1996). Churchill's cognitive and rhetorical style: The debates over Nazi intentions and self-government for India. *Political psychology, 17*, 149-170.

[12] Lewis, C. S. (1952). *Mere Christianity*. New York: Harper Collins.

[13] Chesterton, G. K. (1909). *Orthodoxy*. London: John Lane Company.

[14] Cited in: Oden, T. C., & Crosby, C. (2007). *Ancient Christian Devotional: A Year of Weekly Readings*. Downer's Grove, Illinois: Intervarsity Press.

[15] Chadwick, H. (translator). (1991). *The Confessions of St. Augustine.* New York: Oxford University Press.

[16] Aquinas, T. (1269). *Summa Contra Gentiles, Book III*. Retrieved from: http://www.catholicprimer.org/aquinas/aquinas_summa_contra_gentiles.pdf

[17] Cited in: Chesterton, G. K. (1974). *St. Thomas Aquinas: The Dumb Ox*. New York: Random House.

Chapter 3

[1] From the book: Kurtz, P. (2003). *Science and Religion: Are they compatible?* Prometheus Books: Amherst, NY.

[2] From the book: Kurtz, P. (2003). *Science and Religion: Are they compatible?* Prometheus Books: Amherst, NY.

[3] From the book: Kurtz, P. (2003). *Science and Religion: Are they compatible?* Prometheus Books: Amherst, NY.

[4] From the book: Kurtz, P. (2003). *Science and Religion: Are they compatible?* Prometheus Books: Amherst, NY.

[5] Pelham, B. W., & Blanton, H. (2002). *Conducting research in psychology: Measuring the weight of smoke.* Pacific Grove, CA: International Thompson Publishing.

[6] Ganssle, G. E. (2009). *A reasonable God: Engaging the new face of atheism.* Waco, TX: Baylor University Press.

[7] Cited in: Konner, J. (2007). *The Atheist's Bible: An Illustrious Collection of Irreverent Thoughts.* New York: Harper Collins.

[8] Cited in: Konner, J. (2007). *The Atheist's Bible: An Illustrious Collection of Irreverent Thoughts.* New York: Harper Collins.

[9] For evidence based on psychology research, see: Hauser, M. (2006). *Moral minds: How nature designed our universal sense of right and wrong.* New York: Harper Collins.

[10] For a subjective review of moral overlap of multiple cultural systems, see: Lewis, C. S. (1943). *The abolition of man.* Oxford: Oxford University Press.

[11] For example, see: Conway, L. G., III, Bongard, K., Plaut, V. C., Gornick,L. J., Dodds, D., Giresi, T., Tweed, R. G., Repke, M. A., & Houck, S. C. (2017). Ecological origins of freedom: Pathogens, heat stress, and frontier topography predict more vertical but less horizontal governmental restriction. *Personality and Social Psychology Bulletin.* Advance online publication. DOI: 10.1177/0146167217713192

[12] Barret, H. C., Bolyanatz, A., Crittenden, A. N., Fessler, D. M. T., Fitzpatrick, S., Gurven, M., Henrich, J., Kanovsky, M., Kushnick, G., Pisor, A., Scelza, B. A., Stich, S., von Rueden, C., Zhao, W., & Laurence, S. (2016). Small-scale societies exhibit fundamental variation in the role of intentions in moral judgment. *PANAS, 113*, 4688-4693.

[13] Reyna, C., Tucker, A., Korfmacher, W., & Henry, P. J. (2005). Searching for common ground between supporters and opponents of affirmative action. *Political Psychology, 26*, 667-682.

[14] See Dijksterhuis, A., & Nordgren, L. F. (2006). A theory of unconscious thought. *Perspectives on Psychological Science, 1*, 95-109.

[15] See Gigerenzer, G., & Goldstein, D. G. (1996). Reasoning the fast and frugal way: Models of bounded rationality. *Psychology Review, 103,* 650-669.

[16] In Morris, T. V. (1994). *God and the Philosophers.* Oxford: Oxford University Press.

[17] Pelham, B. W., & Blanton, H. (2002). *Conducting research in psychology: Measuring the weight of smoke.* Pacific Grove, CA: International Thompson Publishing.

[18] Chesterton, G. K. (1974). *St. Thomas Aquinas: The Dumb Ox.* New York: Random House.

[19] Polikinghorne, J. (2008). *Quantum Physics and Theology: An Unexpected Kinship.* London: Society for Promoting Christian Knowledge.

[20] Barker, Dan (2016). *God: The Most Unpleasant Character in All Fiction.* New York: Sterling Press.

[21] For a summary, see: Houck, S. C., Conway, L. G., III, & Gornick, L. J. (2014). Automated integrative complexity: Current challenges and future directions. *Political Psychology, 35,* 647-659.

[22] Cited in: Oden, T. C., & Crosby, C. (2007). *Ancient Christian Devotional: A Year of Weekly Readings.* Downer's Grove, Illinois: Intervarsity Press.

[23] For example, see: Sagar, H. A., & Schofield, J. W. (1980). Racial and behavioral cues in Black and White children's perceptions of ambiguously aggressive acts. *Journal of Personality and Social Psychology, 39*, 590-598.

Chapter 4

[1] Cited in: Oden, T. C., & Crosby, C. (2007). *Ancient Christian Devotional: A Year of Weekly Readings.* Downer's Grove, Illinois: Intervarsity Press.

[2] Cited in: Oden, T. C., & Crosby, C. (2007). *Ancient Christian Devotional: A Year of Weekly Readings.* Downer's Grove, Illinois: Intervarsity Press.

[3] For example, see: Leung, K., & Bond, M. H. (2004). Social axioms: A model for social beliefs in multi-cultural perspective. In M. P. Zanna (ed.), *Advances in Experimental Social Psychology* (vol. 36, pp. 119-197). San Diego: Elsevier Academic Press.

---

[4] For an overview, see: Baumeister, R. F. (2002). Religion and psychology: Introduction to the special issue. *Psychological Inquiry, 13*, 165-167.

[5] Hitchens, C. (2007). *god is Not Great: How Religion Poisons Everything.* New York: Twelve Books.

[6] Russell, B. (1967). *Why I am Not A Christian.* New York: Simon and Schuster.

[7] Stenger, V. J. (2012). *God and the Folly of Faith: The Incompatibility of Science and Religion.* Amherst, NY: Prometheus Books.

[8] Dennett, D. C. (2007). *Breaking the Spell: Religion as a Natural Phenomenon.* New York: Penguin Books.

[9] Cited in: Huberman, J. (2006). *The Quoteable Atheist: Ammunition for Non-Believers, Political Junkies, Gadflies, and Those Generally Hell-bound. New York*: Nation Books.

[10] Cited in: Konner, J. (2007). *The Atheist's Bible: An Illustrious Collection of Irreverent Thoughts.* New York: Harper Collins.

[11] Cited in: Brainyquotes (2017). Retrieved from: https://www.brainyquote.com/quotes/quotes/c/clarenceda383571.html

[12] For example, see: Conway, L. G., III, & Schaller, M. (2005). When authority's commands backfire: Attributions about consensus and effects on deviant decision making. *Journal of Personality and Social Psychology*, *89*, 311-326.

[13] For example, see: Conway, L. G. III, Salcido, A., Gornick, L. J., Bongard, K. A., Moran, M., & Burfiend, C. (2009). When self-censorship norms backfire: The manufacturing of positive communication and its ironic consequences for the perceptions of groups. *Basic and Applied Social Psychology, 31*, 335-347.

[14] For a review, see: Knowles, E. S., & Linn, J. A. (2004). The importance of resistance to persuasion. In E. S. Knowles and J. A. Linn (Eds.), *Resistance and persuasion* (pp. 3-9). Mahwah, NJ: Mahwah Press.

[15] For example, see: Jacks, J. Z., & Devine, P. G. (2000). Attitude importance, forewarning of message content, and resistance to persuasion. *Basic and Applied Social Psychology, 22*, 19-29.

[16] For a review, see: Conway, L. G., III, Houck, S. C., & Gornick, L. J. (2014). Regional differences in individualism and why they matter. In P. J. Rentfrow (Ed.), *Geographical Psychology: Exploring the Interaction of Environment and Behavior* (pp. 31-50). Washington, DC: American Psychological Association.

[17] See also: Conway, L. G., III, Bongard, K., Plaut, V. C., Gornick,L. J., Dodds, D., Giresi, T., Tweed, R. G., Repke, M. A., & Houck, S. C. (2017). Ecological origins of freedom: Pathogens, heat stress, and frontier topography predict more vertical but less horizontal governmental restriction. *Personality and Social Psychology Bulletin*. Advance online publication. DOI: 10.1177/0146167217713192

[18] See Schwartz, B. (2004). *The paradox of choice: Why more is less.* New York: Harper Perennial.

[19] Chesterton, G. K. (1910). *What's Wrong With the World.* New York: Dodd, Mead, & Company.

[20] For a review, see: Finn, C. E. (2017). Why are schools still peddling the self-esteem hoax? *Education Weekly.* Retrieved from: http://www.edweek.org/ew/articles/2017/06/21/why-are-schools-still-peddling-the-self-esteem.html

[21] Laham, S. M. (2012). *The Science of Sin: The Psychology of the Seven Deadlies (and Why They Are So Good For You).* New York: Random House.

[22] For example, see Taylor, S. E., & Brown, J. D. (1988). Illusion and well-being: A social psychological perspective on mental health. *Psychological Bulletin, 103*, 193-210.

[23] See, for example, Krueger, J. I., Vohs, K. D., & Baumeister, R. F. (2008). Is the allure of self-esteem a mirage after all? *American Psychologist, 63*, 64-65.

[24] Baumeister, R.F. (1993) (Ed.). *Self-esteem: The puzzle of low self-regard.* New York: Plenum.

[25] Baumeister, R. F., & Tierney, J. (2011). *Willpower: Rediscovering the greatest human strength.* New York: Penguin Press.

[26] Chesterton, G. K. (1909). *Orthodoxy.* London: John Lane Company.

[27] Chadwick, H. (translator). (1991). *The Confessions of St. Augustine.* New York: Oxford University Press.

[28] Wilde, O. (1986). *The Picture of Dorian Gray.* New York: Penguin Books.

[29] Cited in: Goodreads (2017). Retrieved from: https://www.goodreads.com/quotes/18052-when-i-read-about-the-evils-of-drinking-i-gave

[30] Russell, B. (1967). *Why I am Not A Christian.* New York: Simon and Schuster.

[31] Chesterton, G. K. (1909). *Orthodoxy.* London: John Lane Company.

[32] Shaw, G. B. (1912). *Androcles and the Lion (Preface).* Retrieved from: http://www.gutenberg.org/files/4004/4004-h/4004-h.htm

[33] Cited in: Goodreads (2017). Retrieved from: http://www.goodreads.com/quotes/116680-organized-religion-is-a-sham-and-a-crutch-for-weak-minded

[34] Cobb, M. & Nelson, J. Y. (2011). *Kung Fu Panda II.* United States: Dreamworks.

[35] Schaller, M. (1997). The psychological consequences of fame: Three tests of the self-consciousness hypothesis. *Journal of Personality, 65*, 291-309.

[36] Hull, J. G., & Young, R. D. (1983). Self-consciousness, self-esteem, and success-failure as determinants of alcohol consumption in male social drinkers. *Journal of Personality and Social Psychology,* 44, 1097-1109.

[37] For a review, see: Tweed, R. G., & Conway, L. G., III (2009). Personal resilience in the midst of crisis: Empirical findings from positive psychology. *LCC Liberal Arts Studies, 2*, 25-43.

[38] Seligman, M. E. P., Steen, T. A., Park, N., & Peterson, C. (2006). Positive psychology progress: Empirical validation of interventions. *American Psychologist, 60*, 410-421.

[39] Huta, V., & Ryan, R. M. (2010). Pursuing pleasure or virtue: The Differential and overlapping well-being benefits of hedonic and eudaimonic motives. *Journal of Happiness, Studies, 11*: 735-762.

[40] Pressman, S. D., Kraft, T. L., & Cross, M. P. (2015). It's good to do good and receive good: The impact of a "pay it forward" style kindness intervention on giver and receiver well-being. *The Journal of Positive Psychology, 10*, 293-304.

[41] Kasser, T., & Ryan, R. M. (1993). A dark side of the American dream: Correlates of financial success as a central life aspiration. *Journal of Personality and Social Psychology, 61*, 410-422.

[42] See, for example: Earp, B. D., & Trafimow, D. (2015). Replication, falsification, and the crisis of confidence in social psychology. *Frontiers in Psychology*, Vol. 6, Article 621, 1-11.

[43] For data and a historical overview, see: Earp, B. D., & Trafimow, D. (2015). Replication, falsification, and the crisis of confidence in social psychology. *Frontiers in Psychology*, Vol. 6, Article 621, 1-11.

[44] Earp, B. D., & Trafimow, D. (2015). Replication, falsification, and the crisis of confidence in social psychology. *Frontiers in Psychology*, Vol. 6, Article 621, 1-11.

[45] Lilienfeld, S. O., & Ammirati, R. (2014). Would the world be better off without religion? A skeptic's guide to the debate. *Skeptical Inquirer, 38.4*. Retrieved from: https://www.csicop.org/si/show/would_the_world_be_better_off_without_religion_a_skeptics_guide_to_the_deba

[46] Sheiman, B. (2009). *An Athiest Defends Religion: Why Humanity Is Better Off with Religion Than Without It.* New York: Penguin.

[47] Jones, C. (1966). *How the Grinch Stole Christmas.* United States: Cat in the Hat Productions.

[48] Cited in: Konner, J. (2007). *The Atheist's Bible: An Illustrious Collection of Irreverent Thoughts.* New York: Harper Collins.

Chapter 5

[1] Cited in: Oden, T. C., & Crosby, C. (2007). *Ancient Christian Devotional: A Year of Weekly Readings.* Downer's Grove, Illinois: Intervarsity Press.

[2] Cited in: Oden, T. C., & Crosby, C. (2007). *Ancient Christian Devotional: A Year of Weekly Readings.* Downer's Grove, Illinois: Intervarsity Press.

[3] Cited in: Oden, T. C., & Crosby, C. (2007). *Ancient Christian Devotional: A Year of Weekly Readings.* Downer's Grove, Illinois: Intervarsity Press.

---

[4] For a discussion, see: Heine, S. J., Prouix, T., & Vohs, K. D. (2006). The meaning maintenance model: On the coherence of social motivations. *Personality and Social Psychology Review, 10,* 88-110.

[5] For empirical validation, Dennett refers the reader to Pew Research Center, http:/people-press.org/.

[6] BBC (2003). The Big Read: Top 100. *BBC Home.* Retrieved from: http://www.bbc.co.uk/arts/bigread/top100.shtml

[7] Cited in: Konner, J. (2007). *The Atheist's Bible: An Illustrious Collection of Irreverent Thoughts.* New York: Harper Collins.

[8] Cited in: Konner, J. (2007). *The Atheist's Bible: An Illustrious Collection of Irreverent Thoughts.* New York: Harper Collins.

[9] Cited in: Konner, J. (2007). *The Atheist's Bible: An Illustrious Collection of Irreverent Thoughts.* New York: Harper Collins.

[10] Cited in: Ask Atheists (2016). *Top quotes.* Retrieved from http://www.askatheists.com/atheist-quotes

[11] Cited in: Ask Atheists (2016). *Top quotes.* Retrieved from http://www.askatheists.com/atheist-quotes

[12] Cited in: Ask Atheists (2016). *Top quotes.* Retrieved from: http://www.askatheists.com/atheist-quotes

[13] Cited in: Goodreads (2017). Retrieved from: https://www.goodreads.com/author/quotes/1194.Richard_Dawkins?page=2

[14] From the book: Kurtz, P. (2003). *Science and Religion: Are they compatible?* Prometheus Books: Amherst, NY.

[15] Durant, W. (2002). *The Greatest Minds and Ideas of All Time.* New York: Simon & Schuster.

[16] Hart, M. H. (1992). *The 100: A Ranking of the Most Influential Persons in History.* New York: Hart Publishing.

[17] 4Mind4Life (2008). List of Top 50 Geniuses. *4Mind4Life Blog*. Retrieved from: http://4mind4life.com/ blog/2008/03/30/list-of-geniuses-top-50-influential-minds/

[18] Chadwick, H. (translator). (1991). *The Confessions of St. Augustine*. New York: Oxford University Press.

[19] Chesterton, G. K. (1910). *What's Wrong With the World*. New York: Dodd, Mead, & Company.

[20] Lewis, C. S. (1960). *Miracles*. London & Glasgow: Collins/Fontana.

[21] Dictionary of the Christian Church. (2005). *Apostle's Creed*. Oxford: Oxford University Press.

[22] Cited in: Konner, J. (2007). *The Atheist's Bible: An Illustrious Collection of Irreverent Thoughts*. New York: Harper Collins.

[23] Dawkins, R. (2004). *The ancestor's tale: A pilgrimage to the dawn of evolution*. London: Weidenfeld & Nicolson.

[24] Flew, A. & Varghese, R. A. (2007). *There is a God: How the World's Most Notorious Atheist Changed His Mind*. New York: Harper Collins.

[25] Conway, L. G. III. (2011). From the classic dumb professor vault: Is God only an illusion in your brain? *Apologetic Professor*. Retrieved from: http://www.apologeticprofessor.com/articles/?s=vanderbilt

[26] Collins, F. S. (2006). *The Language of God: A Scientist Presents Evidence for Belief*. New York: Free Press.

[27] For discussion, see: Intrepid Muses (2014). About the big bang and fundamentalists. *Intrepid Muses Blog*. Retrieved from: https://intrepidmuses.wordpress.com/2014/05/17/about-the-big-bang-and-fundamentalists/

[28] Dawkins. R. (1995). *River out of Eden: A Darwinian View of Life*. New York: Basic Books.

[29] Dawkins, R. (1998). *Unweaving the Rainbow: Science, Delusion and the Appetite for Wonder*. New York: Houghton Mifflin.

[30] Munafo, R. (2016). All-time top 232 movies by U.S. theatre attendance. Retrieved from: http://www.mrob.com/pub/film-video/topadj.html

[31] The Street (2017). So how many people watched Super Bowl 51? Retrieved from: https://www.thestreet.com/video/13991608/so-how-many-people-watched-super-bowl-51.html

[32] FIFA (2015). *2014 FIFA World Cup reached 3.2 billion viewers, one billion watched final. Retrieved from http://www.fifa.com/worldcup/news/y=2015/m=12/news=2014-fifa-world-cuptm-reached-3-2-billion-viewers-one-billion-watched--2745519.html*

[33] Cited in: Brainyquotes (2017). Retrieved from: https://www.brainyquote.com/quotes/quotes/m/michaeljor447194.html?src=t_sports

[34] Cited in: Brainyquotes (2017). Retrieved from: https://www.brainyquote.com/quotes/quotes/s/stephenmr728540.html?src=t_sports

[35] For a review, see: Smith, E. R., & Mackie, D. M. (2007). Social psychology (3rd edition). New York: Psychology Press.

[36] Taylor, Henry (2012). Jedi' religion most popular alternative faith. *The Daily Telegraph.* London: Telegraph Media Group.

[37] Buchanan, R. T. (2015). Thousands of Turkish students sign petition to build Jedi Temple on university campus. *The Independent.* Retrieved from: http://www.independent.co.uk/news/world/thousands-of-turkish-students-sign-petition-to-build-jedi-temple-on-university-campus-10161225.html

Chapter 6

[1] Cited in Barker, Dan (2016). *God: The Most Unpleasant Character in All Fiction.* New York: Sterling Press.

[2] Ask Atheists (2016). *Top quotes.* Retrieved from http://www.askatheists.com/atheist-quotes

[3] Cited in: Goodreads (2017). Retrieved from: https://www.goodreads.com/quotes/20655-god-is-a-comedian-playing-to-an-audience-that-is

[4] Ask Atheists (2016). *Top quotes.* Retrieved from http://www.askatheists.com/atheist-quotes

[5] Cited in: Konner, J. (2007). *The Atheist's Bible: An Illustrious Collection of Irreverent Thoughts*. New York: Harper Collins.

[6] Lewis, C. S. (1966). *Letters of C.S. Lewis*. New York: Harper Collins.

[7] Daily Atheist Quotes (2013). *Carl Sagan*. Retrieved from: http://dailyatheistquote.com/atheist-quotes/2013/08/06/your-god-is-too-small-for-my-universe/

[8] Cited in: Hitchens, C. (2007). *The Portable Atheist: Essential Readings for the Non-Believer*. Philadelphia: Da Capo Press.

[9] For discussion, see: Conway, L. G., III, Conway, K. R., Gornick, L. J., & Houck, S. C. (2014). Automated integrative complexity. *Political Psychology, 35*, 603-624.

[10] Chadwick, H. (translator). (1991). *The Confessions of St. Augustine*. New York: Oxford University Press.

[11] Cited in: Oden, T. C., & Crosby, C. (2007). *Ancient Christian Devotional: A Year of Weekly Readings*. Downer's Grove, Illinois: Intervarsity Press.

[12] Armenian Church Library (2017). *Nicene Creed*. Retrieved from: http://www.armenianchurchlibrary.com/files/creed.pdf

[13] See also: Placher, W. C. (1988). *Readings in the History of Christian Theology*. Philadelphia: The Westminster Press.

[14] Cited in: Oden, T. C., & Crosby, C. (2007). *Ancient Christian Devotional: A Year of Weekly Readings*. Downer's Grove, Illinois: Intervarsity Press.

[15] Cited in: Oden, T. C., & Crosby, C. (2007). *Ancient Christian Devotional: A Year of Weekly Readings*. Downer's Grove, Illinois: Intervarsity Press.

[16] Cited in: Oden, T. C., & Crosby, C. (2007). *Ancient Christian Devotional: A Year of Weekly Readings*. Downer's Grove, Illinois: Intervarsity Press.

[17] Cited in: Oden, T. C., & Crosby, C. (2007). *Ancient Christian Devotional: A Year of Weekly Readings*. Downer's Grove, Illinois: Intervarsity Press.

[18] Armenian Church Library (2017). *Nicene Creed*. Retrieved from: http://www.armenianchurchlibrary.com/files/creed.pdf

[19] Cited in: Oden, T. C., & Crosby, C. (2007). *Ancient Christian Devotional: A Year of Weekly Readings.* Downer's Grove, Illinois: Intervarsity Press.

[20] Cited in: Oden, T. C., & Crosby, C. (2007). *Ancient Christian Devotional: A Year of Weekly Readings.* Downer's Grove, Illinois: Intervarsity Press.

[21] Bloom, P. (2016). *Against Empathy: The Case for Rational Compassion.* New York: Harper-Collins.

[22] Bloom, P. (2016). *Against Empathy: The Case for Rational Compassion.* New York: Harper-Collins.

[23] For example, see: Toi, M., & Batson, C. D. (1982). More evidence that empathy is a source of altruistic motivation. *Journal of Personality and Social Psychology, 43*, 281-292.

[24] Bloom, P. (2016). *Against Empathy: The Case for Rational Compassion.* New York: Harper-Collins.

[25] Barker, Dan (2016). *God: The Most Unpleasant Character in All Fiction.* New York: Sterling Press.

[26] Cited in: Konner, J. (2007). *The Atheist's Bible: An Illustrious Collection of Irreverent Thoughts.* New York: Harper Collins.

[27] Toi, M., & Batson, C. D. (1982). More evidence that empathy is a source of altruistic motivation. *Journal of Personality and Social Psychology, 43*, 281-292.

[28] Thesaurus.com. (2017). *Empathy: Synonyms.* Retrieved from: http://www.thesaurus.com/browse/empathy

[29] Cited in: Barker, Dan (2016). *God: The Most Unpleasant Character in All Fiction.* New York: Sterling Press.

[30] Conway, L. G., III. (2013). Why was the cross necessary? *Apologetic Professor.* Retrieved from http://www.apologeticprofessor.com/articles/2013/09/why-was-the-cross-necessary/

[31] Tolkien, J. R. R. (1954). *The Lord of the Rings: The Two Towers.* London: George Allen & Unwin.

[32] Baumeister, R.F., & Leary, M.R. (1995). The need to belong: Desire for interpersonal attachments as a fundamental human motivation. *Psychological Bulletin, 117*, 497-529.

[33] Smith, E. R., & Mackie, D. M. (2007). *Social psychology (3rd edition).* New York: Psychology Press.

Chapter 7

[1] Cited in: Brainyquotes (2017). Retrieved from: http://www.brainyquote.com/quotes/quotes/d/davidducho474091.html

[2] Cited in: Solomon, D. (2005). Bill Cosby's not funny. *New York Times.* Retrieved from: http://www.nytimes.com/2005/03/27/magazine/bill-cosbys-not-funny.html

[3] For discussion, see Kitayama, S., Conway, L. G., III, Pietromonaco, P.R., Park, H., & Plaut, V. C. (2010). Ethos of independence across regions in the United States: The production-adoption model of cultural change. *American Psychologist, 65*, 559-574.

[4] Hitchens, C. (2007). *god is Not Great: How Religion Poisons Everything.* New York: Twelve Books.

[5] Hitchens, C. (2007). *god is Not Great: How Religion Poisons Everything.* New York: Twelve Books.

[6] Hitchens, C. (2007). *god is Not Great: How Religion Poisons Everything.* New York: Twelve Books.

[7] Leary, M. R., Tambor, E. S., & Terdal, S. K., & Downs, D. L. (1995). Self-esteem as an interpersonal monitor: The sociometer hypothesis. *Journal of Personality and Social Psychology, 68*, 518-530.

[8] Brewer, M. B. (1991). The social self: On being the same and different at the same time. *Personality and Social Psychology Bulletin, 17*, 475-482.

[9] Cited in: Brainyquotes (2017). Retrieved from: http://www.brainyquote.com/quotes/quotes/j/jonathansa485191.html

[10] Lewis, C. S. (1952). *Mere Christianity.* New York: Harper Collins.

[11] For example, see: Paulhus, D. L. (1998). Interpersonal and intrapsychic adaptiveness of trait self-enhancement: A mixed blessing? *Journal of Personality and Social Psychology, 74*, 497-1197-1208.

[12] Bushman, B. J., & Baumeister , R. F. (1998). Threatened egotism, narcissism, self-esteem, and direct and displaced aggression: Does self-love or self-hate lead to violence? *Journal of Personality and Social Psychology, 75*, 219-229.

[13] Cited in: Oden, T. C., & Crosby, C. (2007). *Ancient Christian Devotional: A Year of Weekly Readings*. Downer's Grove, Illinois: Intervarsity Press.

[14] Chesterton, G. K. (1910). *What's Wrong With the World.* New York: Dodd, Mead, & Company.

[15] From Aristotle (350 BC). *Politics*. Translated by Benjamin Jowett. Retrieved from: http://classics.mit.edu/Aristotle/politics.html

[16] For example, see: Conway, L. G., III, Clements, S. M., & Tweed, R. G. (2006). Collectivism and governmentally initiated restrictions: A cross-sectional and longitudinal analysis across nations and within a nation. *Journal of Cross-Cultural Psychology, 37*, 1-23.

[17] Chesterton, G. K. (1910). *What's Wrong With the World.* New York: Dodd, Mead, & Company.

[18] Cited in: Oden, T. C., & Crosby, C. (2007). *Ancient Christian Devotional: A Year of Weekly Readings*. Downer's Grove, Illinois: Intervarsity Press.

Chapter 8

[1] Barker, Dan (2016). *God: The Most Unpleasant Character in All Fiction*. New York: Sterling Press.

[2] Barker, Dan (2016). *God: The Most Unpleasant Character in All Fiction*. New York: Sterling Press.

[3] Barker, Dan (2016). *God: The Most Unpleasant Character in All Fiction*. New York: Sterling Press.

[4] Barker, Dan (2016). *God: The Most Unpleasant Character in All Fiction*. New York: Sterling Press.

[5] Lewis, C. S. (1952). *Mere Christianity*. New York: Harper Collins.

For More Books & Resources, please visit:
TheDramaticPen.com and LifesMidterm.com.

www.ingramcontent.com/pod-product-compliance
Lightning Source LLC
Chambersburg PA
CBHW060323030426
42336CB00011B/1185
* 9 7 8 1 6 4 1 5 7 0 0 0 8 *